MW01295063

AIR CRASH INVESTIGATIONS

LACK OF EXPERIENCE

The Crash of a Maryland State Police Helicopter

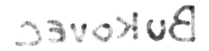

AIR CRASH INVESTIGATIONS

Over the last decades flying has become an every day event, there is nothing special about it anymore. Safety has increased tremendously, but unfortunately accidents still happen. Every accident is a source for improvement. It is therefore essential that the precise cause or probable cause of accidents is as widely known as possible. It can not only take away fear for flying but it can also make passengers aware of unusual things during a flight and so play a role in preventing accidents.

Air Crash Investigation Reports are published by official government entities and can in principle usually be down loaded from the websites of these entities. It is however not always easy, certainly not by foreign countries, to locate the report someone is looking for. Often the reports are accompanied by numerous extensive and very technical specifications and appendices and therefore not easy readable. In this series we have streamlined the reports of a number of important accidents in aviation without compromising in any way the content of the reports in order to make the issue at stake more easily accessible for a wider public.

Allistair Fitzgerald, editor.

AIR CRASH INVESTIGATIONS

LACK OF EXPERIENCE

The Crash of a Maryland State Police Helicopter

Allistair Fitzgerald, editor.

MABUHAY PUBLISHING

AIR CRASH INVESTIGATIONS

LACK OF EXPERIENCE

The Crash of a Maryland State Police Helicopter

Crash During Approach to Landing of Maryland State Police Aerospatiale SA365N1, N92MD District Heights, Maryland, September 27, 2008. National Transportation Safety Board Accident Report NTSB/AAR-09/07 PB2009-910407

All Rights Reserved © 2012, by Allistair Fitzgerald, editor
allistair_fitzgerald@yahoo.com

No part of this book may be reproduced or transmitted in any form or by any means, graphic, electronic, or mechanical, including photocopying, recording, taping, or by any information storage retrieval system, without the permission in writing from the publisher.

A Lulu.com imprint

ISBN: 978-1-300-53101-2

Executive Summary

On September 27, 2008, about 2358 eastern daylight time, an Aerospatiale (Eurocopter) SA365N1, N92MD, call sign Trooper 2, registered to and operated by the Maryland State Police (MSP) as a public medical evacuation flight, impacted terrain about 3.2 miles north of the runway 19R threshold at Andrews Air Force Base (ADW), Camp Springs, Maryland, during an instrument landing system approach. The commercial pilot, one flight paramedic, one field provider, and one of two automobile accident patients being transported were killed. The other patient being transported survived with serious injuries from the helicopter accident and was taken to a local hospital. The helicopter was substantially damaged when it collided with trees and terrain in Walker Mill Regional Park, District Heights, Maryland. The flight originated from a landing zone at Wade Elementary School, Waldorf, Maryland, about 2337, destined for Prince George's Hospital Center, Cheverly, Maryland. Night visual meteorological conditions prevailed for the departure; however, Trooper 2 encountered instrument meteorological conditions en route to the hospital and diverted to ADW. No flight plan was filed with the Federal Aviation Administration (FAA), and none was required. The MSP System Communications Center (SYSCOM) was tracking the flight using global positioning system data transmitted with an experimental automatic dependent surveillance-broadcast communications link.

The National Transportation Safety Board determined that the probable cause of this accident was the pilot's attempt to regain visual conditions by performing a rapid descent and his failure to arrest the descent at the minimum descent altitude during a nonprecision approach. Contributing to the accident were (1) the pilot's limited recent instrument flight experience, (2) the lack of adherence to effective risk management procedures by the MSP, (3) the pilot's inadequate assessment of the weather, which led to his decision to accept the flight, (4) the failure of the Potomac Consolidated Terminal Radar Approach Control (PCT) controller to provide the current ADW weather observation to the pilot, and (5) the increased workload on the pilot due to inadequate FAA air traffic control handling by the Ronald Reagan National Airport Tower and PCT controllers.

The safety issues discussed in this report involve risk assessments, pilot performance and training, terrain awareness and warning systems, air traffic control deficiencies, SYSCOM duty officer performance, and emergency response. Also discussed are patient transport decisions, flight recorder requirements, and FAA oversight. Safety recommendations concerning these issues are addressed to the FAA, the MSP, Prince George's County, all public helicopter emergency medical services operators, and six other organizations whose members are involved in search and rescue activities.

9

Contents:

CHAPTER 1

FACTUAL INFORMATION

History of Flight

On September 27, 2008, about 2358 eastern daylight time,[1] an Aerospatiale (Eurocopter) SA365N1, N92MD, call sign Trooper 2, registered to and operated by the Maryland State Police (MSP) as a public medical evacuation (medevac) flight,[2] impacted terrain about 3.2 miles north of the runway 19R threshold at Andrews Air Force Base (ADW), Camp Springs, Maryland, during an instrument landing system (ILS)[3] approach. The commercial pilot, one flight paramedic (medic), one field provider,[4] and one of two automobile accident patients being transported were killed. The other patient

---

[1] Unless otherwise indicated, all times are eastern daylight time based on a 24-hour clock.
[2] On March 13, 2009, the Federal Aviation Administration issued a memorandum classifying the accident flight as a public aircraft operation.
[3] The ILS is a precision approach system that consists of a localizer and a glideslope, which provide lateral and vertical guidance, respectively, to help the pilot align with the runway.
[4] The field provider was a local emergency medical technician who was brought aboard the helicopter at the automobile accident site. When two patients are carried, a field provider is needed to assist the flight paramedic.

being transported survived with serious injuries from the helicopter accident and was taken to a local hospital. The helicopter was substantially damaged when it collided with trees and terrain in Walker Mill Regional Park, District Heights, Maryland.

The flight originated from a landing zone at Wade Elementary School, Waldorf, Maryland, at 2337, destined for Prince George's Hospital Center (PGH), Cheverly, Maryland. Night visual meteorological conditions (VMC) prevailed for the departure; however, Trooper 2 encountered instrument meteorological conditions (IMC) en route to the hospital and diverted to ADW. A flight plan was not filed with the Federal Aviation Administration (FAA), and none was required. The MSP System Communications Center (SYSCOM) was tracking the flight using global positioning system (GPS) data transmitted via an experimental automatic dependent surveillance-broadcast (ADS-B) [5] communications link.

Review of SYSCOM audio recordings revealed that the SYSCOM duty officer (DO) received the medevac flight request at 2301:51. The pilot of Trooper 2, located at ADW, was notified of the flight at 2302:13 by the DO. The pilot asked where the flight was, and the DO responded that it was in Waldorf. The pilot stated, —I don't know if we can get to the hospital, to which the DO responded, —well that's fine, if you can't make the mission you can't make the mission. The pilot continued, —they say College Park is 800 feet up there [6] …that is only a mile north of the hospital, ah PG [Prince George's] is on fly by anyway.‖ [7] The DO subsequently confirmed that the hospital was no longer —on fly by, and the pilot

---

[5] ADS-B is a surveillance system in which an aircraft is fitted with cooperative equipment in the form of a data link transmitter. The aircraft periodically broadcasts its GPS-derived position and other information, such as velocity, over the data link, which is received by a ground-based transceiver for use by air traffic control and other users.

[6] The cloud ceiling at College Park Airport was 800 feet. The cloud ceiling is the height above the ground of the base of the lowest layer of cloud covering more than half the sky.

[7] According to MSP personnel, —PG on fly by meant the hospital was full to incoming patients by air.

responded, —ok, we can give it a shot. After a brief conversation regarding the coordinates of the landing zone, the pilot stated, —maybe they will change their mind. The DO responded —well hold on, they ain't going to change their mind, if you tell them you will go, they want you to go…that's up to you, do you think you can fly it? The pilot again stated that the ceiling at College Park Airport was 800 feet and added that the ceiling at Ronald Reagan Washington National Airport (DCA) was 1,200 feet. Additionally, the pilot remarked that he had just heard a medevac helicopter operated by a private company complete an interhospital transfer flight in the same area, and then said, —if they can do it we can do

it. The DO responded, —ok it is up to you, and the pilot subsequently stated, —yeah we ought to be able to do it…we're going to try it. Trooper 2 departed ADW at 2310:22 to the automobile accident site to pick up the two patients. (See figure 1) The flight arrived at the landing zone about 2319 and departed about 2337 with the patients and the field provider aboard.

Review of FAA air traffic control (ATC) radio recordings revealed that the pilot of Trooper 2 contacted DCA tower at

2337:45, reporting his departure from Waldorf en route to PGH. The tower controller approved the operation. ATC radar and ADS-B data indicated that Trooper 2 entered the Washington class B airspace [8] about 2341 at an altitude of 1,000 feet mean sea level (msl) on a northerly heading.

During the initial contact with Trooper 2, the DCA tower controller provided a pilot report from another helicopter [9] that had —...passed through the highway 210/295 area 30 minutes earlier, describing cloud bases at 900 feet that lowered further north. About 2344:23, the pilot reported that —...we just ran into some heavy stuff—I don't think we're gonna be able to make it all the way to the hospital. I'd like to continue on about three more miles and see what happens, and if I don't see a hole I'll have to go IFR [instrument flight rules] back to Andrews. The controller advised the pilot that he could choose an altitude at his discretion and to advise of his intentions. Trooper 2 continued on a northerly heading at an altitude of 900 feet msl, and, about 2347, reached a point about 0.25 miles east of PGH. The pilot then began a 180° right turn.

About 2347:28, Trooper 2 advised the DCA tower controller, —it's solid up here. I'd like to climb to 2,000 feet and go over to radar and shoot an approach over at Andrews. The controller responded, —Trooper 2 approved as requested, contact approach on...118.95. There was no subsequent coordination about Trooper 2 between the DCA controller and the Potomac Consolidated Terminal Approach Control (PCT) controller.

---

[8] Class B airspace surrounds the nation's busiest airports, typically extending from the surface to 10,000 feet. An ATC clearance is required for all aircraft to operate in the area.

[9] This was the private medevac helicopter that the pilot referred to in his prelaunch conversation with the DO. This helicopter transferred a patient to Washington Hospital Center in Washington, D.C., from a hospital in La Plata, Maryland. La Plata is located about 6 miles south of the automobile accident site.

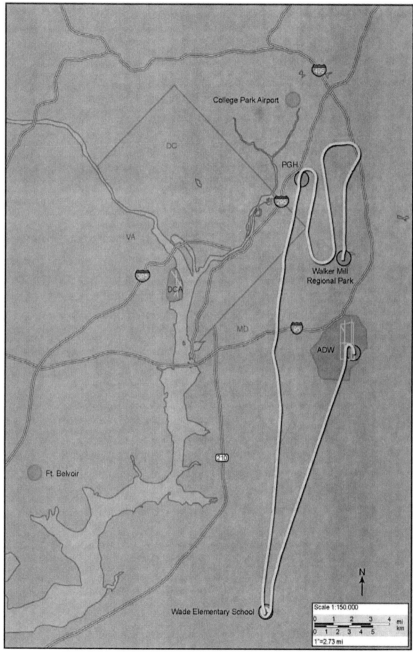

Figure 1. Trooper 2 ground track indicated by white line.

About 2348:01, Trooper 2 called PCT, the controller acknowledged, and at 2348:08 the pilot stated, —*we tried to make a medevac up at PG hospital, we're about 7 miles northwest of Andrews, like to climb to 2,000 feet and shoot an approach to runway 1L at Andrews.* The controller did not respond. At 2349:15, Trooper 2 called PCT again, the controller responded, and the pilot stated, —*Yes sir, I was waiting for a reply. Climbing to 2,000 feet and my course is uh...200 degrees.* The controller responded, —*All right Trooper 2 present position 200 degrees is approved the altimeter 2991 Washington tower 120.75.* The pilot replied, —*No sir, I want to shoot the approach at Andrews.* The controller then transmitted, —*All right tell you what go direct to the you—you want to shoot the ILS 19 what runway?* The pilot asked, —*Are they using 19? Uh, runway 19R.*

At 2350:01, the controller began vectoring Trooper 2 to the ILS approach for runway 19R. (See figure 2 on the following page.) After some discussion, the pilot stated that he wanted a single approach to a full stop at Andrews to drop off patients aboard. At 2351:49, the PCT approach controller advised Trooper 2 that —the latest weather at Andrews is 7 miles uh 1,800 broken and the temperature uh right now is uh 21 dew point [10] 19. [11] The pilot acknowledged.

Vectoring to final approach continued, and at 2353:46 the approach controller transmitted, —*Trooper 2 mile and a half from the final approach fix turn right heading 1 uh 70 maintain 2000 until you're established on the localizer cleared ILS 1R [sic] approach into Andrews.* At the time, Trooper 2 was crossing to the east side of the localizer, and the 170° heading issued would not have resulted in a successful

---

[10] Dew point is the temperature to which air must be cooled in order to be saturated with water vapor already in the air. The difference between the actual air temperature and the dew point is called the temperature/dew point spread. As the spread narrows, relative humidity increases, and relative humidity is 100 percent when the temperature and the dew point are the same.
[11] Subsequent review of ADW weather reports showed that the weather information provided to the pilot had been issued at 1855 local time, and was almost 5 hours old.

intercept. Review of radar data indicated that the pilot continued the turn to approximately 210°, which resulted in intercepting the localizer about 1 mile from the final approach fix. The controller asked Trooper 2 to report that the flight was established on the localizer, and the pilot did so. The pilot was then instructed to contact ADW tower.

About 2355:12, Trooper 2 checked in with ADW, stating, —*Trooper 2's with you off uh on the localizer for runway 19R.* At this time, the helicopter was 6 nautical miles from the 17 runway, at an altitude of 1,900 feet msl. The ADW controller responded, —*Trooper 2 roger runway 19[unintelligible] cleared for the option* [12] *wind 090 at 5.* About 2356:45, Trooper 2 reported, —*I'm not picking up the glideslope.* The controller replied, —*it's showing green on the panel but you're the only aircraft we've had in a long time so I don't really know if it's working or not.* About 2357:00, Trooper 2 requested an airport surveillance radar (ASR) approach, [13] but the ADW controller replied that she was not current to provide that service. [14] There were no further communications with Trooper 2. The last radar target for Trooper 2 was detected about 23:57:50, at 800 feet msl over Walker Mill Regional Park. The last ADS-B target for Trooper 2 was detected about 2358:04, at 325 feet msl near the accident site. Table 1 shows a timeline of the accident sequence.

---

[12] Cleared for the option is ATC authorization for an aircraft to make a touch-and-go, low-approach, missed-approach, stop-and-go, or full-stop landing at the discretion of the pilot.

[13] An ASR approach is an approach wherein the air traffic controller instructs the pilot, based on aircraft position in relation to the final approach course and the distance from the end of the runway as displayed on the controller's radarscope.

[14] The FAA requires controllers to complete three ASR approaches every quarter, including one no-gyro approach, to remain current (qualified) for that type of approach.

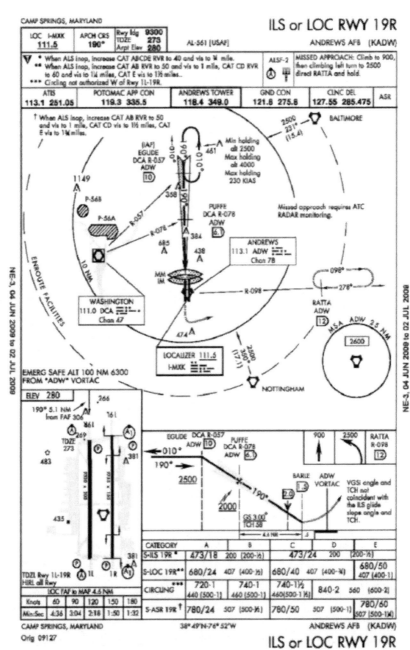

Figure 2. ILS runway 19R published approach chart.

Table 1. Timeline of Events.

Time (EDT)	Event	Elapsed Time Since Helicopter Dispatched
22:45:34	First of numerous 911 calls made to Charles County communications about the auto accident	---
22:46:09	First group of fire department personnel arrived on-scene	---
23:01:51	Charles County called SYSCOM to request helicopter transport for two patients to PGH	---
23:02:13	SYSCOM called Trooper 2 (T2) and asked if they could accept mission; T2 accepted	00:00:00
23:10:32	T2 radioed SYSCOM en route to landing zone	00:08:19
23:20:50	T2 arrived at landing zone	00:18:37
23:36:56	T2 departed with 2 patients and field provider	00:34:43
23:37:30	T2 radioed SYSCOM en route to PGH; 8 minute estimated time en route with 2 patients	00:35:17
23:44:23	Pilot of T2 reported to DCA "...we just ran into some heavy stuff" and stated he would continue for about 3 miles and if he "didn't see a hole," he would "go IFR" to ADW.	00:42:10
23:47:29	Pilot of T2 reported to DCA "it's solid up here" and requested an instrument approach at ADW. At this time, T2 was about 0.25 miles east of PGH.	00:45:15
23:58:00	ACCIDENT	00:55:47

The accident occurred about 3.2 miles from the threshold of runway 19R and along the extended runway centerline. The wreckage was found in a heavily wooded area of Walker Mill Regional Park at an elevation of about 200 feet msl. Figure 3 on the following page shows an aerial photo of the park.

Figure 3. Aerial photograph of Walker Mill Regional Park, overlaid with the locations of Trooper 2.

Injuries to Persons

Table 2. Injury Chart.

Injuries	Flight Crew	Other Crew	Passengers	Other	Total
Fatal	1	2	1	0	4
Serious	0	0	1	0	1
Minor	0	0	0	0	0
None	0	0	0	0	0
Total	1	2	2	0	5

Damage to Aircraft

The helicopter sustained extensive structural damage, separated components, and broken main rotor blades.

Other Damage

No other damage was reported.

Personnel Information

The pilot, age 59, held a commercial pilot certificate issued on June 28, 1979, with ratings for rotorcraft-helicopter and instrument helicopter. He also held a private pilot certificate with a rating for single-engine, land airplanes. In addition, the pilot held a flight instructor certificate initially issued on August 20, 1985, and most recently renewed on October 27, 2007, with ratings for rotorcraft-helicopters and instrument helicopters. The pilot was issued a second-class medical certificate on September 26, 2008, with the restriction —must wear corrective lenses.‖

The pilot was hired by MSP as a state trooper on January 5, 1970, applied for a position in the aviation division on May 29, 1979, and began employment in that division on July 15, 1981. All of the pilot's flight experience was accumulated as an MSP employee.

The pilot's most recent annual MSP flight evaluation was conducted on October 27, 2007. This evaluation was completed in 1.6 hours of flight time and included an instrument proficiency check (IPC), a biennial flight review, and a re-instatement of the pilot's flight instructor certificate. During the IPC portion of the flight, the pilot performed two approaches to runway 1L at ADW, an ILS approach and a non-precision approach. [15] According to the instructor who flew with the pilot, his instrument skills were —slightly above average when compared to other pilots. The pilot received his MSP —Command Instrument Single Pilot Certification during this evaluation and was signed off to act as —Single Pilot PIC [pilot-in-command] for IFR Operations, which allowed him to file a flight plan and fly in IMC, if necessary, to fly a patient to a trauma center, reposition the helicopter to a maintenance facility, return to base from a flight, or conduct a VIP (very important person) transport. [16]

The pilot's most recent IPC (which included training) was completed on May 13, 2008. This training included 1 hour of ground instruction and 1.4 hours of flight instruction. According to the pilot's training folder, he conducted an ILS approach and a non-precision approach at ADW and a GPS approach at St. Mary's County Airport, Leonardtown, Maryland. The paperwork did not specify which ILS approach at ADW was performed; however, it stated both approaches were practiced coupled and uncoupled with the autopilot. According to the instructor pilot, there was nothing unusual about the flight and the pilot —did pretty well. He additionally reported that the accident pilot was —above average compared to other pilots and had —no trouble with instrument approaches.

---

[15] A nonprecision approach is a standard instrument approach procedure in which no electronic glideslope is provided.
[16] MSP pilots who have not received —Command Instrument Single Pilot Certification may not file and fly in IMC; they are signed off for —Single Pilot PIC IFR Operations (Recovery Only).

Review of the pilot's logbook revealed that he had 5,225.1 total flight hours of which 2,770 hours were in the accident make and model helicopter. The pilot had recorded 5,200.9 hours as PIC and 1,919.9 hours of night flight time. His last recorded night flight was on September 16, 2008. The pilot's total instrument flight experience is unknown. [17] In the year prior to the MSP's change in their instrument training program, [18] the pilot logged instrument time on 7 flights, accumulating 6.2 hours of instrument time and completing 20 approaches. After the change and in the year prior to the accident, the pilot logged instrument time on only 2 flights, which included 2.1 hours of instrument time and 4 instrument approaches. The pilot's most recent flight at night under instrument conditions took place on October 29, 2006, and the pilot completed 3 instrument approaches and logged 0.5 hours of simulated instrument time. During the 2 years preceding the accident, the pilot completed 25 instrument approaches: 20 approaches at ADW, 3 GPS approaches at nearby airports, and 2 unspecified approaches in a simulator. Out of the 20 ADW approaches, only 4 were nonprecision approaches. The nonprecision approaches practiced did not include the localizer approach to runway 19R. The pilot's last recorded instrument flight was on May 13, 2008, during his IPC. However, a medic reported that, a few days before the accident, the pilot practiced a GPS approach in VMC conditions for proficiency purposes during his return to base after a medevac flight.

MSP reported that the pilot was off duty for 2 days before the accident and scheduled to work the late shift (1900 to 0700) on the day of the accident. The pilot's wife reported that he slept normally on the 2 days before the accident, waking between 0800 and 0830 and going to bed between midnight and 0100. On the day of the accident, the pilot woke about 0800 and reported for work about 1800 in preparation for his 1900 start of duty. The pilot's wife

---

[17] The pilot logbook examined by NTSB investigators was labeled ―logbook #3‖and covered the period from June 17, 2006, to September 13, 2008. The pilot's family was unable to locate previous logbooks. There were no carried-over flight times listed for simulated or actual instrument experience.
[18] See later section for a discussion of MSP's instrument training program.

indicated that his activities and demeanor in the days before the accident were routine.

According to his most recent airman's physical examination, the pilot was 6 foot 3 inches tall and weighed 293 pounds (resulting in a body mass index (BMI) of 36.6). [19] His wife stated that the pilot had snored his entire adult life, and a colleague stated that he was notorious among coworkers for loud snoring. Obesity and snoring are two symptoms of obstructive sleep apnea, a disorder in which an individual's airway is repeatedly blocked during sleep, usually by soft tissue collapsing at the back of the throat. [20] Interruptions in breathing can cause hypoxia, disturbed sleep architecture, and decrements in cognitive and psychomotor functioning. [21]

Aircraft Information

The Aerospatiale SA365N1 —Dauphin helicopter has twin engines, a single main rotor, and a retractable tricycle landing gear. As shown in figure 4 below, the helicopter has four doors, two on each side. The four-bladed main rotor is mounted on the main gearbox, which is directly above the cabin. Two Turbomeca Arriel 1C1 engines are mounted side by side aft of the main gearbox. The accident helicopter was equipped with two front seats with dual controls and an aftermarket medical interior including four seats and two litters.

---

[19] BMI is a person's weight in kilograms divided by his or her height in meters squared. The National Institutes of Health defines a person with a BMI of 30 or more as obese.

[20] See, for example, O. Resta, et al., —Sleep-Related Breathing Disorders, Loud Snoring and Excessive Daytime Sleepiness in Obese Subjects, International Journal of Obesity and Related Metabolic Disorders, vol. 25, no. 5 (2001), pp. 669-75.

[21] See, for example, L. Ferini-Strambi, et al., —Cognitive Dysfunction in Patients with Obstructive Sleep Apnea (OSA): Partial Reversibility after Continuous Positive Airway Pressure (CPAP),‖Brain Research Bulletin, vol. 61, no. 1 (2003), pp. 87-92.

Figure 4. Photograph of an exemplar Aerospatiale SA365N1 helicopter.

The transport-category helicopter was manufactured in 1988. At the time of the accident, the helicopter had flown 8,869.1 total flight hours and had 34,575 total landings. The helicopter was equipped with a night vision imaging system, which was used for law enforcement flights and was not being used during the accident flight; a radar altimeter; 22 and an autopilot that was capable of fully coupling to an ILS. The helicopter was not equipped with a terrain awareness and warning system (TAWS).

The helicopter had a standard airworthiness certificate and was being maintained in accordance with Eurocopter's recommended maintenance service requirements, using an approved aircraft inspection program. According to the aircraft logbook, a 100-hour airframe and engine inspection was accomplished on

---

22 A radar altimeter uses the reflection of radio waves from the ground to determine the height of an aircraft above the surface.

September 22, 2008, 3.2 flight hours before the accident. The No. 1 (left) and No. 2 (right) engines had accumulated calculated total times of 7,077.3 and 7,426.5 flight hours, respectively, at the time of the accident. The No. 1 and No. 2 engines had accumulated 1,120 and 574.7 hours since overhaul, respectively.

An aircraft weight and balance form was completed prior to departure for the flight. According to the form, the helicopter departed ADW on the flight with 1,180 pounds of fuel. National Transportation Safety Board (NTSB) investigators estimated the fuel weight on board at the time of the accident was close to 880 pounds. Given these fuel weights, the helicopter was within weight and center of gravity limits throughout the flight.

According to MSP Aviation Command personnel, the instrument approach charts were in a pouch on the right side of the pilot's seat, readily accessible to the pilot.

Meteorological Information

There is an Automated Surface Observing System (ASOS) at ADW. Observations are augmented and verified by Air Force personnel who are qualified weather observers. The ASOS was in augmented mode at the time of the accident. [23]

The 2255 September 27, 2008, surface weather observation at ADW was wind 110° at 3 knots, visibility 7 miles, ceiling broken clouds at 1,300 feet, temperature 20° C, dew point 20° C, and altimeter setting 29.92 inches of mercury (Hg).

The 2355 surface weather observation at ADW was wind 080° at 3 knots, visibility 4 miles in mist, scattered clouds at 200 feet, ceiling broken clouds at 500 feet, temperature 20° C, dew point 20° C, and altimeter setting 29.91 inches of Hg.

---

[23] Augmentation is the process of adding information from a trained weather observer to that which is observed automatically.

The 0055 September 28, 2008, surface weather observation at ADW was wind 070° at 3 knots, visibility 4 miles in mist, ceiling broken clouds at 200 feet, overcast at 500 feet, temperature 20° C, dew point 20° C, and altimeter setting 29.91 inches of Hg.

Visibility at ADW was reported to deteriorate rapidly after 0117, with visibility dropping to 1/4 mile at 0137.

The fire chief on duty at ADW around the time of the accident indicated that the weather had been —foggy and —soupy, with estimated visibilities at 1/4 mile and, in some places, less. However, he stated that, at the time, he could see the high intensity lights on the hangars on the opposite side of the field, about 1 mile from his location. The fire chief noted that, at the north end of the airport, the visibility was slightly better and he could see down to Suitland Parkway, which was about 1/2 mile from his location. The chief also noted that, about 2250, he was standing about 200 feet from the 13-story ADW tower [24] and said that the top of the cab was—shrouded in fog.

A homeowner who resided about 1.8 miles southwest of the accident site, stated that, between 2345 and 2400, he heard a helicopter approaching his home and that it flew over his house flying towards Walker Mill Regional Park and ADW. He went outside and observed the helicopter below the clouds in a descending attitude; he estimated the clouds were 100 to 150 feet above the trees. He stated that it was dark and there was a light mist of rain. He observed the helicopter until it disappeared from view.

Preflight Weather Information

About 1851, when the pilot began his shift, he obtained and printed a weather briefing from the FAA's Direct User Access Terminal (DUAT) service. [25] The information that the pilot obtained included trend weather observations, pilot reports, weather radar data, terminal forecasts, and wind aloft forecasts. The 1755 ADW surface weather observation and the ADW terminal forecast were included in the information. The 1755 surface weather observation at ADW was wind 090° at 5 knots, visibility 7 miles, a few clouds at 1,000 feet, temperature 21° C, dew point 20° C, and altimeter setting 29.90 inches of Hg. The ADW terminal forecast valid from 1800 on September 27, 2008, to 0100 on September 28 indicated wind 120° at 6 knots, visibility 7 miles, and scattered clouds at 2,000 feet. Between 0100 and 0200, the weather at ADW was expected to become wind variable at 6 knots, visibility 3 miles in mist, ceiling broken at 500 feet and overcast at 1,000 feet. The included DCA terminal forecast issued at 1330 indicated that by 2200 the weather was expected to be wind 150° at 5 knots, visibility 5 miles in light rain showers and mist, scattered clouds at 400 feet and ceiling overcast at 800 feet. There is no record of any further contacts with DUAT before the accident.

The 1851 DUAT briefing did not include weather hazards because the pilot did not select them from the DUAT menu of products. If the pilot had included weather hazards, the briefing would have contained an Airman's Meteorological Information (AIRMET) for IFR conditions issued at 1645 and valid until 2300 that forecast ceilings below 1,000 feet and visibilities less than 3 miles in precipitation and mist for an area that began immediately north and east of ADW, extending over eastern Maryland, Delaware, eastern Pennsylvania, New Jersey and New England. [26]

An amended terminal forecast for DCA, issued at 1933, indicated that from 2000 on September 27, 2008, to 0200 on September 28, the weather was expected to be wind 70° at 3 knots, visibility greater than 6 miles, ceiling broken at 1,500 feet, broken

---

[24] The height of the ADW tower is 181 feet.

[25] The DUAT service provides direct access to weather briefings, flight planning, and flight plan filing.

[26] AIRMETs are weather advisories issued concerning weather phenomena that are of operational interest to all aircraft and potentially hazardous to aircraft having limited capability because of lack of equipment, instrumentation, or pilot qualifications. An AIRMET for IFR conditions is issued when ceilings of less than 1,000 feet and/or visibilities less than 3 miles are forecast to affect a widespread area.

PGH was located within the boundaries of the AIRMET; ADW and the landing zone at Waldorf were not.

An amended terminal forecast for DCA, issued at 1933, indicated that from 2000 on September 27, 2008, to 0200 on September 28, the weather was expected to be wind 70° at knots, visibility greater than 6 miles, ceiling broken at 1,500 feet, broken clouds at 25,000 feet. Between 2000 and 2300, temporary changes were expected to visibility 3 miles in light rain showers, ceiling broken at 800 feet, overcast at 1,500 feet.

A new AIRMET for IFR conditions was issued at 2245 and was valid until September 28, 2008, at 0500 and forecast ceilings below 1,000 feet, visibilities less than 3 miles in precipitation, and mist for an area that encompassed Maryland, the District of Columbia, and Virginia. The entire route of flight of Trooper 2 was located within the boundaries of the new AIRMET.

The MSP Aviation Command has access to the helicopter emergency medical services (HEMS) weather tool. [27] FAA Notice N 8000.333 describes the HEMS tool and explains that it is an experimental product. The notice states, with regard to Part 135 HEMS operators:

> The only approved use of this Tool is in VFR operations and then only in the context of supporting a —no-go decision. Operators may not use the tool as the sole source for decisions to —Go. They may only use established primary products such as METARs [meteorological aerodrome reports], TAFs [terminal aerodrome forecasts], area forecasts, weather depiction charts, prognosis charts, etc., to make both —Go and —No-Go decisions.

After the accident, another pilot, who arrived at the hangar

---

[27] At the request of the FAA, the National Weather Service's Aviation Digital Data Service development team created a tool specifically designed to show weather conditions for the short-distance and low-altitude flights that are common for the HEMS community

about 0310 on September 28, the morning after the accident, noted that the pilots' computer was on and the HEMS weather tool was on the screen. He stated that most pilots read the weather directly from the HEMS weather tool before a flight. The SYSCOM DO stated that when he came on duty about 1800 on day of the accident, the HEMS weather tool indicated marginal visual flight rules (VFR) conditions throughout most of the state. [28] He noted that all MSP aviation bases were operating under a flight-by-flight (—call by call‖) [29] conditional response due to the weather conditions throughout the state.

The HEMS weather tool is capable of displaying surface weather observations, terminal area forecasts, AIRMETs and pilot reports. Since HEMS weather tool data are not archived, it is impossible to confirm which of these items the pilot may have chosen to display. Surface weather observations for ADW, DCA, Fort Belvoir, Virginia, and College Park, Maryland, are normally available through the HEMS weather tool. Figure 1 shows the locations of these surface weather observation sites. About 2300, the HEMS weather tool would have displayed the 2252 DCA observation [30] indicating 10 miles visibility and multiple cloud layers, with the lowest layer a few clouds at 1,400 feet, and the 2250 College Park observation [31] indicating visibility of 10 miles and ceiling 800 feet overcast. Because of a technical failure in Department of Defense (DoD) communications, the current

---

[28] According to National Weather Service definitions, IFR conditions prevail when visibility is less than 3 miles and ceiling is less than 1,000 feet. Marginal VFR prevails when visibility is 3 to 5 miles and ceiling is 1,000 to 3,000 feet. VFR prevails when visibility is greater than 5 miles and ceiling is greater than 3,000 feet.

[29] When an MSP section is —call by call, the reported or observed weather is close to MSP VFR weather minimums.

[30] The 2252 surface weather observation at DCA was wind calm, visibility 10 miles, a few clouds at 1,400 feet, 3,000 feet scattered, 11,000 feet scattered, ceiling 25,000 feet broken, temperature 22° C, dew point 19° C, altimeter setting 29.92 inches of Hg.

[31] The 2250 surface weather observation at College Park was wind calm, visibility 10 miles, ceiling 800 feet overcast, temperature and dew point 21° C, altimeter setting 29.92 inches of Hg.

surface observations for ADW and Fort Belvoir were not available at 2300. The 2255 ADW observation was indicating visibility 7 miles and ceiling broken at 1,300 feet, and the 2255 Fort Belvoir observation [32] was indicating visibility 1 1/4 miles in mist and a few clouds at 15,000 feet.

Department of Defense Weather Dissemination

According to U.S. Air Force personnel, a data communications switch failure at Offutt Air Force Base, Nebraska, prevented the Air Force Weather Agency (AFWA) from transmitting military alphanumeric data to the National Weather Service (NWS). This prevented the display of military surface weather observations, including ADW ASOS observations, on non-DoD weather outlets, such as DUAT and the HEMS weather tool. On September 27, 2008, the last ADW observation noted on non-DoD weather outlets was for 1855, about 5 hours before the accident. Local dissemination of the ADW ASOS observations to the ADW tower was not affected.

Replacement of the switch restored transmission capability. The outage of the circuit between the NWS and the AFWA lasted about 18 hours and 33 minutes. [33] There was no backup procedure available to continue transmission of weather data during the outage. As of April 29, 2009, a backup procedure had been developed, tested, and implemented that would provide for the uninterrupted exchange of data between AFWA and NWS during a failure of this type.

---

[32] The 2255 surface weather observation at Fort Belvoir was wind calm, visibility 1 1/4 miles, mist, a few clouds at 15,000 feet, temperature and dew point 20° C, altimeter setting 29.91 inches of Hg.

[33] The NWS reported the outage was from 1922 on September 27, 2008, to 1355 on September 28, 2008.

Runway Visual Range Information

The runway visual range (RVR) [34] sensors along ADW runway 19R began reporting touchdown values below 6,000 feet about 40 minutes before the accident. Touchdown RVR values below 2,400 feet were reported from about 11 minutes before the accident through the time of the accident.

According to FAA equipment logs, the edge and approach lights for runway 19R were set to their lowest intensity, step 1, while Trooper 2 was on approach. Step 1 is the normal setting at night when the visibility is above 5 miles. [35] According to FAA technicians, because the RVR system measures the distance along the runway that the edge lights are visible, the reported value changes when the lights are turned up or down. When the edge lights are set to the lowest two settings, reported RVR values are not considered accurate and do not necessarily represent a specific level of fog or other obstruction to visibility.

The ADW tower controller stated that the RVR display in the tower was not on because it is ADW practice not to activate the RVR display until the official weather observer reports visibility of 1 mile or less. The controller was therefore unaware of the RVR values detected by the system and did not increase the runway light intensity setting to get an accurate RVR value.

Aids to Navigation

FAA technicians conducted a postaccident certification of the ILS for runway 19R on September 28, 2008, and found all certification parameters to be within tolerances. A flight check was

---

[34] The RVR is the measurement of the visibility near the runway's surface. The measurement represents the horizontal distance that a pilot should be able to see down a runway from the approach end.

[35] A high-intensity runway lighting system has 5 intensity steps. Step 1 is the lowest intensity, and step 5 is the highest. When visibility is less than 3 miles, the normal setting is at least 3. Settings are under the control of the tower.

conducted on September 29, 2008, and the system was again within tolerances. Review of maintenance and monitoring logs for the ILS for runway 19R showed no unusual maintenance or malfunctions recorded for the system.

Communications

There were no known difficulties with communications equipment.

Airport Information

ADW is owned and operated by the US Air Force. The ADW tower is operated by the FAA. [36] The airport is located about 3 miles east of Camp Springs, Maryland, at an elevation of 280 feet. ADW has two runways: 1R/19L and 1L/19R. Runway 1L/19R is 9,300 feet long and 200 feet wide with a concrete surface. Runway 19R is equipped with a high-intensity approach lighting system with centerline-sequenced flashers; high-intensity runway edge lights; and a touchdown, midpoint, and rollout RVR system. The runway's touchdown zone elevation is 273 feet.

Instrument Approach Procedures

There are 12 instrument approach procedure charts published for ADW. The ILS runway 19R approach and the localizer runway 19R approach are presented on a single approach chart, as shown in figure 2. The ILS runway 19R approach procedure requires aircraft to intercept and track the inbound localizer course of 190°, fly level until the glideslope is intercepted, and then descend along the glideslope. If the pilot does not see the runway environment or the runway by the time the aircraft reaches the decision altitude of 473 feet msl, which is 200 feet above the runway touchdown zone elevation, the pilot is required to perform a

---

[36] The Federal Aviation Act of 1958 mandated that certain military bases, including ADW, have FAA-staffed control towers. The FAA has been operating the tower at ADW since 1961.

missed approach.

According to the FAA's *Aeronautical Information Manual* Section 1-1-9 (j), when the glideslope fails, the ILS reverts to a nonprecision localizer approach. The localizer runway 19R approach procedure requires the aircraft to pass over the final approach fix, which is located 6.1 distance-measuring-equipment (DME) [37] miles from the ADW VORTAC. [38] After passing over the final approach fix, the pilot can descend to the minimum descent altitude (MDA) of 680 feet msl which is 407 feet above the runway touchdown zone elevation. The pilot cannot descend below the MDA unless the runway environment or the runway is visible. If the runway environment or the runway is not visible when the aircraft reaches the missed approach point, which is located 1.5 DME miles north of the ADW VORTAC, the pilot is required to perform a missed approach. [39]

The approach chart also provides the ASR runway 19R approach's MDA, which is 780 feet msl, or 507 feet above the runway touchdown zone elevation. According to information in the FAA's Instrument Flying Handbook and Aeronautical Information Manual, the procedure for an ASR approach, usually called a surveillance approach, requires the controller to provide radar vectors to establish the aircraft on the final approach path. The controller then advises the pilot of the published MDA and missed approach point and then instructs the pilot when to begin descent to the MDA. On final approach, the controller provides vectors to keep the aircraft tracking on the extended runway centerline and advises the pilot of the distance from the missed approach point at

[37] Distance measuring equipment is a pulse-type electronic navigation system that shows the pilot, by an instrument panel indication, the number of nautical miles between the aircraft and a ground station.

[38] A VORTAC is a ground station that transmits navigation signals whereby the pilot of an aircraft equipped with appropriate receivers can determine distance and bearing to the station.

[39] The ADW VORTAC is located near the middle of the airport. When an aircraft reaches the missed approach point for the localizer approach to runway 19R, it is 0.5 nautical miles from the runway threshold.

each mile of the final approach. Guidance is provided all the way to the missed approach point where, unless the runway environment or the runway is visible, the pilot is required to perform a missed approach.

Flight Recorders

The helicopter was not equipped, and was not required to be equipped, with a cockpit voice recorder (CVR) or a flight data recorder (FDR).

Wreckage and Impact Information

Examination of the crash site revealed that the helicopter initially collided with the upper section of an 80-foot tree in a level, descending attitude on a heading of 191° magnetic. A debris path approximately 164 feet long extended from this tree to the main wreckage. The helicopter was separated into three main parts and many smaller pieces. All components of the helicopter were accounted for at the accident site. In addition, no evidence was identified of any preimpact mechanical failures or malfunctions of the aircraft's systems or the airframe.

As shown in figure 5 below, the fuselage came to rest on its left side. The right side of the fuselage was crushed and exhibited horizontal scrape marks, and the cabin and cockpit areas were extensively damaged. The right-side pilot's door was located in a tree near the main wreckage.

The radar altimeter bug [40] was set to 300 feet, which is 573 feet above msl at the runway threshold. The horizontal situation indicator on the pilot's side of the instrument panel was set to 190°. Instrument approach charts, including the chart of the ILS runway 19R approach, were found scattered throughout the debris near the nose of the helicopter.

---

[40] The radar altimeter bug is set by the pilot to a preselected altitude, and when the helicopter approaches and descends below that altitude, the radar altimeter generates visual and aural alerts.

Figure 5. Photograph of the accident site.

Medical and Pathological Information

Autopsies were performed on the four fatally injured occupants by the state of Maryland, Office of the Chief Medical Examiner. The cause of death for all four individuals was listed as —multiple injuries.‖

The FAA's Civil Aerospace Medical Institute performed toxicology tests on tissue specimens from the pilot. The results were negative for carbon monoxide, cyanide, ethanol, and a wide range of drugs, including major drugs of abuse. A review of the pilot's FAA airman medical records revealed that his medical certificate had never been suspended, denied, or revoked. According to his wife, the pilot was in good health and had experienced no major changes in health in the past 12 months.

The survivor sustained multiple traumatic injuries from the helicopter accident. She was hospitalized until November 5, 2008, and then discharged to a rehabilitation center. On November 26, 2008, she was discharged to her home.

Fire

No in-flight or postcrash fire occurred.

Survival Aspects

The pilot occupied the right front seat, and the left front seat was vacant. The medic occupied an aft-facing seat positioned just behind and between the two front seats. The field provider occupied a forward-facing seat positioned in the center of the aft bulkhead; the seat consisted of a seat cushion fitted into a depression in the floor and affixed to the aft bulkhead with a Velcro strip. The fatally injured patient was on the primary litter, located on the left side of the helicopter, and the surviving patient was on the secondary litter, located on the right side of the helicopter. The patients were placed onto the litters while already strapped to backboards provided by local emergency medical services (EMS) personnel, and the backboards were secured to the litters.

The pilot's seat was found near its original location in the fuselage and was heavily damaged. The lap belt of the pilot's four-point harness was found buckled, and the webbing had been cut by first responders. Neither shoulder harness fitting was engaged in the central buckle. The aft-facing medic seat was found near its original location in the cabin and was heavily damaged. The four-point restraint for the medic seat was undamaged and unbuckled. The field provider seat cushion was found in the debris near the fuselage. The four-point restraint for the field provider seat was found buckled, and the lap belt and both shoulder harness webbings had been cut by first responders.

The primary litter stayed in place within the cabin. It was undamaged except for a 4-inch section of aluminum plate that was bent upwards on the inboard side. The backboard was found detached from the litter, and the right-side handle at the head end of the board was fractured. The secondary litter was found in the debris field in multiple pieces. The lower portion of the litter was bent upward approximately 90°. The backboard was found detached from the litter, and both of the handles at the toe end of the board were fractured.

Emergency Response

The ADW controller noticed that Trooper 2 was missing almost immediately after radar contact was lost, and she began attempting to contact the pilot. At 2359:50, she also advised the ADW fire department chief, who was expecting to meet the helicopter, that she had lost radar contact with Trooper 2. The chief then contacted the PG County Communications Center and MSP Forestville barrack about the missing helicopter, and he then engaged in a ground search of ADW and the MSP hangar to locate Trooper 2.

The ADS-B trip history report indicated that the SYSCOM DO logged Trooper 2 as landed at ADW at 0002:02. When he received a call at 0014:11 from MSP Forestville inquiring about the whereabouts of Trooper 2, the DO immediately responded, —they landed at Andrews. When informed by MSP Forestville that the ADW tower controller had lost Trooper 2 from radar, [41] he was surprised. He then attempted to contact Trooper 2 by radio and got no response. The DO provided MSP Forestville with Trooper 2's last ADS-B coordinates.

MSP personnel said that the equipment installed on the helicopters for ADS-B tracking—does not function well at low levels. There had been many instances when the ADS-B position stopped at the end of a runway even though the helicopter had actually landed at the other end of the runway or somewhere else. This, they said, led to a —lack of confidence in the low-level

---

[41] MSP Forestville had received this information from the ADW fire chief.

position and to —conditioning among personnel to assume that the helicopter had landed safely when the ADS-B signal was lost.

According to MSP operational policy at the time of the accident, the troopers at each barrack were responsible for managing any incident that happened in their area of responsibility. Therefore, the shift supervisor on duty at the Forestville barrack became the incident commander for the search for the helicopter until the barrack commander arrived about 0100 and took over. The shift supervisor was not familiar with the flightpath to ADW and was unable to tailor the search to the area directly along the flightpath. He sent troopers to check the unpopulated areas that were about 2 miles north of ADW since, as he said in an interview, —all the initial indications were that the helicopter went missing within 2 miles of ADW.(The ADW tower controller had reported that the helicopter was within 2 miles of the airport.) The shift supervisor relied on ADW tower controllers or SYSCOM to provide him with the last known location of the helicopter. However, he said that he did not plot the coordinates that the SYSCOM DO gave him because he did not know —what the coordinates meant.

About 0021:45, the DO provided PG County dispatchers with Trooper 2's last ADS-B coordinates by reading a string of numbers, —three eight five two one seven, north was seven six five two two six. The DO did not indicate that the numbers were in the form of degrees, minutes, seconds. The DO also added that the location of the coordinates was approximately nautical miles southwest of FedEx Field. [42] (See figure 6 below.)

PG County dispatchers responded by sending patrol vehicles to the area southwest of FedEx Field. They also plotted the coordinates using an online mapping program, but the dispatchers assumed the coordinates were in the form of degrees, decimal

---

[42] FedEx Field is a football stadium located in Landover, Maryland, in PG County.

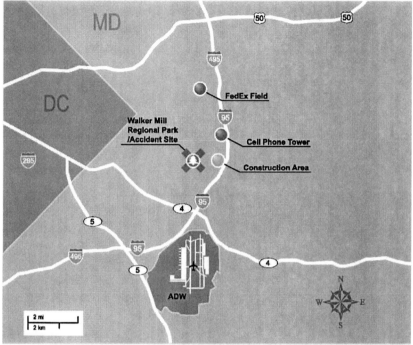

Figure 6. Map of search area (not to scale).

degrees, which they were accustomed to using, so they entered the coordinates in that format. The location returned by the software program was near Calvert Cliffs, Maryland, located about 30 miles southeast of the accident site. This location raised confusion among PG County personnel and, about 0032:02, a county dispatcher called SYSCOM to verify the location. An operator at SYSCOM responded, —okay I don't know where the duty officer got those [coordinates]….The operator did not communicate with the DO to verify the coordinates given to PG County dispatchers. The misunderstanding about the format of the coordinates was not discovered, and confusion about the helicopter being near Calvert Cliffs persisted as the search continued.

During the search, PG County dispatchers initiated an offer to —ping‖the cell phones of the troopers who had been on the helicopter and, thus, to possibly identify their location more accurately. MSP SYSCOM accepted the offer, and at 0036:19, the SYSCOM DO provided two cell phone numbers, one for the pilot and one for the medic. PG County dispatchers contacted the cellular service provider and went through the emergency process of finding the closest cell phone tower. At 0114:47, the cellular provider gave the street address of the tower but did not provide a distance or bearing from the tower. The address was immediately provided to PG County police officers and MSP Forestville, and numerous officers and troopers responded to that location. Approximately 10 minutes later, the Forestville MSP shift commander called PG County dispatchers and discovered that the best search area was probably within a 2- to 3- mile radius of the cellular tower.

Meanwhile, about 0044:42, the medic of Trooper 8, based in Norwood, Maryland, about 20 miles northwest of the accident site, called SYSCOM and requested and received the last known ADS-B coordinates of Trooper 2. The medic stated that since Trooper 8 was —down for weather, [43] he and the Trooper 8 pilot were going to drive to the area where Trooper 2 was thought to have crashed. The medic said in a postaccident interview that he —used the computer and plotted the coordinates near the north entrance to Walker Mill Regional Park. He and the arrived at the park's north entrance about 0100. There were several PG County police officers there, and they heard from them about —pings from one of the trooper's cell phones. Because they believed these —pings were giving a more accurate location, the pilot and the medic left Walker Mill Regional Park and drove to the address provided by the PG County police officers, arriving at a mall parking lot near the cell phone tower.

About 0103:02, the DO called ADW tower and asked the controller for the time of the last contact with Trooper 2. The ADW controller stated that the time was about midnight. The DO asked, —do you have a particular location, a north or west location? The

---

[43] Trooper 8 had been notified by the SYSCOM DO about 0025 that Trooper 2 was missing and requested to launch and head toward ADW. Trooper 8 departed Norwood, encountered low-level clouds about 2 miles south of Norwood, and aborted the flight.

controller responded that she could not provide latitude and longitude coordinates and reported Trooper 2's last known position as 2 miles north of the runway. Again the DO asked, —there's no way to get any kind of a bearing on what his location was, as far as north and west? The ADW controller responded, —I don't know how to do that. [44]

When the MSP Forestville barrack commander arrived at the barrack, she took over from the shift supervisor as the incident commander and set up a command post in the barrack's parking lot. About 0154:39, the barrack commander called MSP Forestville to request an aviation command unit to respond to the command post at Forestville, saying —we've got questions that we need them to answer about how things work.

About 0134, both PG County and MSP search efforts began to focus on a construction area located about 1.25 miles east of the accident site, where a witness reported seeing something come down. Visibility in the unlighted area was reported to be approximately 50 feet. About 0143:37, PG County personnel at the construction area reported needing —true 4-wheel drive vehicles to search the area.

While the search of the construction area was proceeding, the pilot and medic of Trooper 8 met an MSP Aviation Command sergeant who had also responded to the mall parking lot. The sergeant asked them if anyone had talked to ADW tower. About 0142, Trooper 8's pilot called and spoke with the ADW tower controller, who reported losing radar contact with the helicopter about 2 miles out on approach to runway 19R. The pilot took out an ADC map 45 and drew a straight line out from runway 19R; the line intersected with Walker Mill State Park, the same location where Trooper 8's medic had plotted the original coordinates. They immediately drove back to the park, arriving at the south end of the

---

[44] The ADW controller had not received training on how to use a program called CountOps to obtain the coordinates of Trooper 2's last radar position.

park about 0155. About 0158, the two troopers proceeded into the park on foot and located the wreckage and the survivor.

Additional Information on Emergency Response

Interviews with MSP personnel at the Forestville barrack indicated that MSP road troopers performed their daily duties by referencing ADC grid maps and were not aware that those maps contained latitude and longitude coordinates. Some MSP patrol cars were equipped with laptop computers and software that allowed them to enter latitude and longitude coordinates, but none of the troopers interviewed had received any training on how to use this function.

During a postaccident visit to PCT, NTSB investigators were shown an FAA system known as CountOps, an automated traffic count program that tracks the movement of aircraft through PCT airspace. Included in the items recorded by the system is the last observed position of aircraft under PCT control. CountOps was available on the night of the accident and could have been used by either the ADW controller or the operations manager on duty at PCT to obtain the latitude and longitude coordinates for the last radar position of Trooper 2.

When interviewed, the operations manager on duty at PCT stated that he was not familiar with any way to obtain latitude and longitude coordinates for PCT traffic. Also, the location function of CountOps had not been part of training given on the system at ADW, so the ADW controller was unaware of it. Therefore, the system was not consulted during the search for Trooper 2.

---

[45] ADC, of the Langenscheidt Publishing Group, publishes a popular series of maps, atlases, and guidebooks in the Mid-Atlantic region that are often used by Maryland troopers.

Tests and Research

Engine Examinations

The No. 1 and No. 2 engines were examined at the manufacturer's facility. A factory-supplied fuel control unit was installed on each engine, [46] and the engine was run in a test cell. The No. 1 engine was run to 100 percent of the gas-producer turbine's rotational speed (N1). The engine ran with normal fuel consumption and normal oil consumption and did not exhibit any abnormal noises or vibrations.

The No. 2 engine was run to 95 percent of N1. The engine ran with normal fuel consumption and normal oil consumption and did not exhibit any abnormal noises or vibrations. The engine was not run to 100 percent of N1 because multiple sparks were exiting the exhaust pipe. A borescope examination of the turbine assemblies revealed no defects, and the sparks were attributed to wreckage debris passing through the engine.

The No. 1 and No. 2 fuel control units were examined at the manufacturer's facility and run on a test fixture after the impact-damaged parts of their controlling mechanisms were replaced. Both units performed adequately at all ranges of rpm.

Avionics Examinations

The helicopter was equipped with a power analyzer and recorder (PAR) computer, which monitors and records turbine engine parameters for engine health trending and maintenance diagnostics. The PAR computer does not record data continuously; it records data only when certain discrete events occur, including engine starts and stops, engine parameter exceedances, and engine power checks. Examination revealed that the unit was slightly damaged but the internal components were intact. The memory was

---

[46] The fuel control units were replaced as both had sustained impact damage to their controlling mechanisms.

read, and the calibration of the unit was checked and found to be acceptable. The unit recorded no engine exceedances for the flight. The last event recorded was the loss of electrical power to the unit when the accident occurred. The final data recorded included engine torque values of 4.7 percent and 6.8 percent and N1 values of 77.4 percent and 78.4 percent for the left and right engines, respectively. Main rotor speed was recorded at 356 rpm (100 percent rpm); pressure altitude was recorded at 231 feet and indicated airspeed at 92 knots.

The radar altimeter unit, both navigation receivers, both navigation control heads, and the DME transceiver were examined and tested at the manufacturer's facility. The examination revealed no discrepancies that would have prevented them from functioning normally and displaying proper indications during the accident flight. One of the navigation control heads was set to 111.5, the runway 19R localizer frequency. The other was set to 110.5, the runway 19L localizer frequency.

It was not possible to determine the frequency set on the DME transceiver at the time of the accident. Normally, the frequency of the DME transceiver is automatically set to the same frequency as the navigation receiver. However, if the pilot switches the navigation receiver to another frequency but wants to keep the DME on the previous frequency, the pilot can select —HOLD by rotating a spring-loaded switch on the navigation control head. Because the switch springs back to the —ON position when it is released by the pilot, examination of the unit does not reveal whether the pilot selected the hold function.

Aircraft Performance Study

NTSB investigators conducted an aircraft performance study using available ASR, [47]ADS-B, and ATC transcript data. These data

---

[47] ASR systems are short-range (60-nautical-mile) radar systems that produce radar returns every 4.3 to 4.6 seconds for use in providing ATC services.

were used to define the aircraft's flightpath, ground track, ground speed, rate of climb, and ATC communication history. No aircraft acceleration, airspeed, attitude, engine, flight-control input, flight-control surface position, or external atmosphere parameters were recorded in the ADS-B or radar data. Investigators derived true altitude, calibrated airspeed, flightpath angle, estimated bank angle, and true heading parameters.

The calculated Trooper 2 flightpath was compared to the runway 19R calculated glideslope parameters. The initial aircraft descent was consistent with the expected glideslope centerline guidance. About 2357:32, upon reaching an altitude of about 1,450 feet msl on the and a distance of about 4 miles north of the runway threshold, the helicopter's rate of descent increased rapidly from about 500 feet per minute (fpm) to greater than 2,000 fpm, and Trooper 2's flightpath began to deviate below the glideslope. The rapid descent continued until the end of the data.

TAWS Simulation

At the request of NTSB investigators, Honeywell International Inc., a manufacturer of TAWS, used the ADS-B data to calculate the pilot alerts that would be expected if Trooper 2 had been equipped with TAWS. The simulation indicated that, had Trooper 2 been equipped with a Honeywell TAWS system, [48] three terrain alerts would have been generated prior to initial impact, independent of glideslope signal operation. These aural alerts would have been —Caution Terrain, —Warning Terrain, and —Pull-up, given approximately 7, 4, and 2 seconds, respectively, before initial impact with the trees. 49 Additionally, assuming a valid glideslope signal was being received, a —Glideslope aural alert would have been generated approximately 24 seconds before initial impact.

---

[48] The system used was Honeywell's Mark 22 Helicopter Enhanced Ground Proximity Warning System.

[49] The aural alert times from the Honeywell simulation were given in seconds before the end of the ADS-B data, and NTSB investigators correlated the end of the data with the helicopter's initial impact with the trees.

Organizational and Management Information

MSP Aviation Command is composed of eight sections located throughout Maryland. (There are four regions, with two sections in each region.) Aviation Command headquarters is located at Martin State Airport, Middle River, Maryland, collocated with one of the sections. At the time of the accident, MSP operated 12 Aerospatiale AS365 Dauphin helicopters. Trooper 2 was the designation for the helicopter assigned to the MSP Southern Region, Washington Section, located at ADW. The specific (N number) helicopter that flew as Trooper 2 could change from day to day, depending on helicopter availability. At the time of the accident, one helicopter and five pilots were based at Washington Section.

MSP Aviation Command performs medevac, law enforcement, homeland security, search and rescue, and support flights. In calendar year 2007, MSP flew 8,607 flights; 5,769 of those were medevac flights in which a helicopter transported a patient from an accident site to a hospital. The Washington Section completed 1,201 medevac flights to accident sites, 29 interhospital transfers, 155 law enforcement flights, 79 homeland security flights, 50 search and rescue flights, and 122 support flights.

The MSP Aviation Command is funded by the state of Maryland. The state legislature oversees and approves the MSP's budget, considers changes to the program introduced by legislators, and can order audits, conducted by state employees, of specific aspects of the program. However, the state legislature has no direct responsibility for the day-to-day operations of the MSP Aviation Command, nor do they have an aviation surveillance function similar to the FAA.

According to interviews with MSP personnel, funding is independent of the number of flights flown. In the state of Maryland, all requests for medevac flights to accident scenes must be made to MSP first (through SYSCOM), before any private medevac operator. If MSP Aviation Command is not able to respond to a scene for any reason, SYSCOM notifies private medevac operators or other government agencies. [50] When weather is the reason MSP is not able to accept the flight, private operators are generally also required to turn it down. [51] The exception to this is when the weather is a localized phenomenon, for example a thunderstorm, and a private operator has an available helicopter that is not affected by the weather. Private operators based in Maryland primarily perform interhospital patient transports. MSP Aviation Command personnel stated that MSP operates under 14 Code of Federal Regulations (CFR) Part 91 and complies with its requirements pertaining to aircraft and pilot certification, aircraft maintenance, and pilot training. In addition, MSP has implemented a number of policies that mirror 14 CFR Part 135, including use of an operations manual, flight-hour requirements for new pilots, flight-crew duty time limitations, and flight-crew duty rest requirements.

In 2008, the state legislature's Joint Legislative Audit Committee requested that the Office of Legislative Audits conduct an audit of certain aspects of MSP helicopter operations. The scope of the audit included a review of maintenance practices, but it did not include a review of flight operational practices. A report concerning the audit was completed in August 2008 and submitted to the requesting committee. Three of the report's major findings were (1) MSP helicopters were used almost exclusively for critical flights, (2) improved data systems and processes were needed to better manage MSP Aviation Command operations, including helicopter maintenance, and (3) staff turnover issues needed to be addressed.

Does it still need addressed?
+ Pilot revolving door +
Hiring Practice ?   *10/10/2017*
JAB

---

[50] MSP Aviation has memorandums of understanding (MOUs) with each of the three private operators in Maryland, as well as with the U.S. Park Police and the U.S. Coast Guard. They also have a mutual relationship with the Delaware State Police.

[51] MOU's with these organizations reflect this agreement to eliminate pressure to launch.

Training

MSP had three full-time flight instructors at headquarters and four part-time flight instructors in the field, one in each region. Each regional instructor provided recurrent and new-hire training for the seven to eight pilots assigned to their region. The regional instructor for the Southern Region, who had been employed by MSP as a pilot since 1994, stated that, prior to 2000, MSP pilots received —more than enough instrument training. After 2000, however, salaries for helicopter pilots in the civilian industry increased, and a high turnover of pilots began at MSP. The regional instructor stated that, due to the high pilot turnover, —instructors currently spend most of their time training new hires and not enough time performing recurrent training.

On November 27, 2007, MSP Aviation Command changed its instrument training program. Before that date, pilots were required to perform six approaches every 6 months to maintain currency. After that date, pilots would receive two IPCs per year with instructor pilots in order to maintain FAA currency. [52] According to MSP personnel, because MSP normally has just one pilot on duty at each base, the only opportunity pilots had to fly with each other was during a shift change or if they were at headquarters where another pilot might be located. According to the chief pilot, pilots were not conducting —quality training when practicing with other pilots, so he decided to change the training program. He felt that if the pilots flew with instructor pilots, the quality of the training would be better. His goal was to provide a more structured and consistent pilot training plan.

When questioned about the November 2007 change to the instrument training program, the Aviation Command safety officer stated that the change was made for two reasons: to reduce the number of hours the helicopters were flown and to make the

---

[52] Title 14 CFR 61.57 (d), —Recent flight experience: Pilot in command, requires a pilot to perform either 6 approaches during a 6-month timeframe or an IPC in order to maintain FAA currency.

training more consistent. He felt that the new program provided —better quality training. He further stated that before the change, pilots would often perform the six required approaches on the last day of the sixth month —just to document their currency.

The Southern Region instructor reported that the rationale behind the change to the instrument training program was to —save flight time plus it got an instructor in the cockpit. He stated that he did not think two IPCs a year was enough training for pilots to maintain proficiency and that pilots needed to practice more than that. Before the November 2007 change, pilots could practice approaches more often, thus —reinforcing learning.

On September 22, 2008, a pilot from the Cumberland Section sent a memorandum to the MSP Aviation Commander noting hazardous flying conditions in the Cumberland and Frederick sections, due to the mountainous terrain. In the memorandum, the pilot requested that helicopters assigned to these sections be equipped with TAWS. Additionally, he requested:

> Cumberland and Frederick Section pilots should be allowed to resume the previous instrument currency training: six practice or actual approaches every six months. Getting half the previous number of practice approaches and going six months between training opportunities provides neither the frequency nor the quantity of instrument practice needed for this demanding and hazardous flying environment.

The pilot noted that instrument proficiency depended on the quality of initial instrument training, total instrument experience, time elapsed since last instrument experience, and quantity of recent instrument experience.

According to MSP personnel, in response to the pilot's memorandum, the three MSP helicopters with TAWS are now assigned to the Cumberland and Frederick sections whenever possible. Also, in addition to the required IPC every 6 months, pilots with a —Single Pilot PIC for IFR Operations endorsement are encouraged to file an IFR flight plan and fly in IMC whenever possible to maintain their proficiency.

Dispatch System

MSP uses SYSCOM for dispatch and flight-following functions. SYSCOM is a cooperative effort between the Maryland Institute for Emergency Medical Services Systems (MIEMSS) [53] and the MSP. It controls and coordinates all aeromedical emergency responses in Maryland using a 24-hour operations center that provides central aircraft dispatching and emergency communications liaison among 911 centers, police stations or barracks, hospital systems, responding aircraft, and ground units. SYSCOM is staffed at all times with an MSP DO and two communications operators from MIEMSS. The duties of SYSCOM include processing calls, flight tracking, aircraft and crew accountability, and airspace coordination. According to the standard operating procedures, pilots are required to monitor the weather; however, if pilots are unable to obtain a weather update (for example, if they are already on a flight), the DO has access to the HEMS weather tool and may assist pilots. Additionally, the DO is required to obtain a statewide forecast at the beginning of each 12-hour shift (0545 and 1745).

At the time of the accident, SYSCOM DOs were not aviation-trained or certified. They did not have an active role in monitoring weather and determining whether to accept a flight. When a call came into SYSCOM from a 911 center requesting a helicopter transport, the DO notified the closest MSP aviation section. The pilot checked the weather, and the flight crew (pilot and medic) decided whether to accept the flight. If the flight crew accepted the flight, the DO then forwarded the crew flight

---

[53] According to its fact sheet, MIEMSS —oversees and coordinates all components of the statewide EMS educational programs, operates and maintains a statewide communications system, designates trauma and specialty centers, licenses and regulates commercial ambulance services, and participates in EMS-related public education and prevention programs.‖

package and called the requesting 911 center to give them an estimated time of arrival for the helicopter. The flight package typically included incident type, number of patients, approximate age of patients, condition of patients, and landing zone information.

SYSCOM uses ADS-B for tracking and flight following. The data are displayed on a screen at the DO's console and provide status, location, altitude, speed, and course of the aircraft. At the time of the accident, the software provided a view of the ADS-B data over a sectional aeronautical chart. When there was a loss of ADS-B signal, the icon showing the helicopter's last position turned red and there was an audible alert.

In 2005, MSP performed an unannounced training drill for controllers at SYSCOM. In the exercise, a helicopter on a maintenance flight made an unexpected, unannounced landing (not at an airport) while en route to its destination. The goal was to see how and when SYSCOM personnel would ascertain that the helicopter was not where it was supposed to be. The drill identified deficiencies in the situational awareness of the three controllers on duty and led to the reassignment of one individual.

A new operations supervisor was appointed approximately 3 months after that exercise. He concentrated on in-house practice sessions until the new ADS-B system went on line in late 2005. For the next 2 years, the drill procedure involved the selection of a random site for the center's staff to identify. After the geographic target was identified, the staff briefed a response plan. The supervisor noted that these drills —did not involve direct interaction with a flight crew.

Operational Policies

Aviation Command Operational Policies

MSP provided a copy of the Aviation Command Operations Manual dated November 2005. The manual was current at the time of the accident. Under the heading —Flight Crew Responsibilities, the document stated, in part: —Flight crews will call SYSCOM by telephone when they arrive at their office or destination when practical. Under the heading, —Radar Altimeter, the document stated, in part:

> The Decision Height bug will be set on command aircraft Radar Altimeters to an altitude that will provide appropriate response time to alert crew members if they should have an unintentional descent near the water or ground.

> Under the heading —Weather Briefings, the document stated, in part:

> At the beginning of each shift, the pilot will obtain a full weather briefing, to include current and forecasted weather, all NOTAMS [notices to airmen], PIREPS [pilot weather reports] and forecasted winds aloft. In addition to an overall briefing, the pilot will ensure hat he/she gathers information available to make him/her familiar with the weather situations throughout the state, as well as adjoining areas of neighboring states.

> The pilots will obtain, as necessary, sufficient weather information to ensure that the original weather briefing remains valid. The frequency of these additional weather checks will be determined by the severity of the existing or forecasted weather. However, if the section is call by call or weather down, [54] a check of the weather should be conducted at a minimum every two hours.

Under the heading —Aviation Command Weather Minimums for Department Aircraft, the document stated, in part (emphasis in the original):

> No helicopter VFR FLIGHTS will be initiated when the reported or observed weather at the departure, en route and/or destination is below the following:

> 1. Daylight Operations –Sunrise to Sunset if the ceiling is less than 600 feet A.G.L. and/or the visibility is less than two miles.

2. Night Operations —Sunset to Sunrise if the ceiling is less than 800 feet A.G.L. and/or the visibility is less than three miles.

3. In all cases, the helicopter must be capable of maintaining an altitude of at least 500 feet above ground level when operating under VFR, unless otherwise directed by Air Traffic Control or mandated by helicopter route charts.

4. The above minimums are in no way a must respond situation. Each crew will apply the Risk Assessment Matrix as it pertains to Type of Mission Requested, Aircraft MEL [minimum equipment list] Status, All Weather Factors, Terrain the Mission is to be flown over (i.e. mountains), and Human Factors of crew on duty. Based on the crew's Risk Assessment, visibility and/or ceiling minimums will be increased to the crew's comfort level prior to accepting the mission.

SYSCOM Operational Policies

MSP personnel provided an undated document entitled, —SYSCOM Ops Policies 1-08, Joint Operations Center Policy & Procedures DRAFT.‖They explained that this document's draft status was primarily because flight operations policies and procedures in SYSCOM were going through a review and enhancement process. Because MSP Aviation Command believed that many areas would benefit from immediate improvement, they directed the SYSCOM DO to use these policies for normal operations pending the completion of the review. MSP confirmed that the policies included in the document were in place on the night of the accident.

Under the heading, —Flight Tracking, the document stated, in part:

The DO retains responsibility to insure that all MSP Aviation Command helicopters are positively identified & tracked

---

[54] When an MSP section is —weather down, the reported weather is below MSP VFR weather minimums.

throughout each mission. The flight tracking system (ADS-B) vehicle status alert function will remain fully functional at both the DO and SYSCOM-B work stations. This will allow positive status alert monitoring & resets to be completed in the event an operator or DO is temporarily unavailable.

At no time will the audio level on the flight tracking work stations be altered to a point where alerts will not be detected at all stations within the center.

Aircraft ADS-B failures will be identified and confirmed with flight crew.

Loss of ADS-B position reporting will be identified and immediate contact made with flight crew to confirm status.

Under the heading, —Aircraft Emergency, the document stated, in part:

Loss of radio/flight track contact. SYSCOM will confirm aircraft condition, status and position.

b. Establish contact or verify position by available means including ATC if in airport environment, local 911 center if on arrival to field incident.

c. Other radio contact points.

d. Presence of Traffic Information [Service -] Broadcast (TIS[-B]) target visible on last known aircraft heading & alt.[55]

e. DO will initiate emergency services and Command staff alert notifications if unable to confirm position.

f. DO will deploy available MSP and allied resources to assist

---

[55] The Traffic Information Service-Broadcast (TIS-B) is a ground-based broadcast service that provides traffic data derived from secondary surveillance radar. If an aircraft was in radar coverage, but its ADS-B data signal was not being received, a TIS-B data signal would be received over the ADS-B data link system.

assist in aircraft contact and location tasks.

Appendix E of the MSP Aviation Command's Health and Safety Plan contained a—Mishap Plan. The plan provided the SYSCOM DO with a list of information that he was to obtain —upon receiving notification that an aviation related incident/accident has occurred involving [d]epartment personnel, equipment or aircraft. It also provided a list of notifications that the DO was to make. It did not provide the DO any guidance about how to deal with a missing or overdue aircraft.

Appendix D of the Health and Safety Plan contained a —Risk Assessment Matrix that could be used by pilots for flight risk evaluation. However, according to the safety officer, the matrix was not being used by the pilots. The matrix included the statement that it was —designed as a mental guide that is updated prior to flight, during flight and throughout the shift. The safety officer stated that at the time of the accident there was no formal, documented process for pilots to evaluate risk before accepting a flight.

Examination of the matrix revealed that it assigned risk levels of low, medium, and high to various parameters, such as type of flight, weather, and crew rest. For example, under the —Mission Risk category, a night medevac to an accident scene was assigned a low risk level, and under the —Weather Factors category, a dew point/temperature spread of 2° C or less was assigned a medium risk level. The overall risk assessment for a flight was the highest risk level assigned to any category. The matrix indicated that no flights were to be made if the risk level was high but provided no specific guidance concerning what actions should be taken by the pilot if the risk level was medium.

Previous Accidents Involving Maryland State Police

The MSP reported that, since beginning to operate EMS helicopters in 1970, they had experienced five previous accidents, which occurred in 1971, 1972, 1973, 1986, and 1989. The most recent fatal accident occurred on January 19, 1986, when a Bell 206B3 helicopter, registered to and operated by the MSP, impacted terrain in Leakin Park, Baltimore, Maryland. [56] The commercial pilot, who was not instrument rated, and the flight medic were killed, and the helicopter was destroyed. The accident occurred at night when the helicopter was on the return leg of a public medevac flight. The flight encountered IMC, the pilot initiated a 180° turn, and, during the turn, which was made over a dark, wooded area, the helicopter descended and impacted trees and terrain.

After that accident, the MSP took the following corrective actions:

- They replaced their non-IFR certified helicopters with Aerospatiale Dauphin helicopters with single pilot IFR capability.

- Those MSP Aviation Command pilots who were not already instrument rated received the requisite instrument flight instruction and obtained a helicopter instrument rating.

- Minimum requirements of 2,000 rotorcraft flight hours and a helicopter instrument rating became mandatory for all new pilots hired as of January 1, 1987.

Maryland State Police Postaccident Actions

On March 18, 2009, MSP provided a memorandum to the NTSB investigator-in-charge detailing their postaccident actions. These actions included the following:

 - Designing a new mission-specific flight risk assessment tool.

---

[56] The NTSB participated in the investigation of this accident, which was assigned the accident number, BFO86FA014. A probable cause was not determined because, at the time, public aircraft were not within the NTSB's jurisdiction.

- Implementing new weather minimums that delineate cross-country from local flights and mountainous from non-mountainous flights.

- Implementing new training requirements for pilots, including

  - One instrument approach in VMC per month on the return leg of a flight.

  - One instrument approach per month with another check pilot.

  - One training flight with an Aviation Command instructor pilot per year.

  - Two instrument proficiency check flights per year (one every 6 months) with an Aviation Command instructor pilot.

  - One annual evaluation flight with an Aviation Command instructor pilot.

- Training and requiring SYSCOM DOs to be certified flight communicators through the National Association of Air Medical Communication Specialists.

- Training all Aviation Command personnel and MSP field personnel on the use and interpretation of latitude and longitude.

- Resuming unannounced missing aircraft exercises.

During the course of the investigation, NTSB investigators learned of the following additional postaccident changes that were made by MSP:

- When a flight request is received, the DO evaluates the local and regional weather conditions displayed on the HEMS weather tool before allowing the request to proceed to the flight crew or making a no-go decision. The DO can make a no-go decision on a flight request based on weather conditions before the flight crew is notified.

- Flight crews must notify SYSCOM within 5 minutes of landing. If landing confirmation is not received within 5 minutes of the estimated landing time, the DO will attempt to call the aircraft. If there is no contact after 10 minutes, the DO will initiate emergency procedures.

- The software for ADS-B monitoring at all three SYSCOM workstations is capable of overlaying the ADS-B data on ADC street maps, terrain maps, satellite images, and aviation sectional charts.

- The new risk assessment tool assigns low, medium, and high risk levels the colors, yellow, and red, respectively. A percentage, as well as a color, is associated with the operational risk, and there is a range of percentages for green, yellow, and red. Red requires approval from the MSP Director of Flight Operations or a designee before a flight can be accepted. Yellow indicates heightened operational risk, but does not require approval prior to accepting the flight. If the flight crew's operational risk percentage puts the flight request in the —high yellow range for a particular flight request, SYSCOM must be informed by the flight crew that any change during flight, such as deteriorating weather, could put them into the —red and approval would be required to continue the flight or the flight would be cancelled. Moreover, SYSCOM would also notify the requesting agency that the estimated arrival time could be increased and/or the flight cancelled due to an increase in operational risk as determined by the flight crew.

Federal Aviation Administration Oversight

During the NTSB's February 2009 public hearing on the safety of HEMS operations, [57] FAA representatives testified that, with the exception of operations within the National Airspace System, the FAA has no statutory authority to regulate public aircraft operations. Title 49 United States Code (U.S.C.) Section 44701 is the primary authority for federal aviation regulations. This section instructs the FAA administrator to —promote the safe flight of civil aircraft in air commerce through regulations and standards prescribed in the interest of safety. Unless a government-owned (public) aircraft is engaging in a civil operation, it is not subject to civil aircraft and pilot requirements pertaining to certification, maintenance, and training.

FAA Order 8900.1, [58] Chapter 14, Section 2 Public Aircraft Operations and Surveillance Government Aircraft Operations Versus Civil Aircraft Operations, dated September 13, 2007, states that —government-owned aircraft operators holding any type of FAA certification will be included in the normal surveillance activities such as spot inspections of the aircraft and aircraft records. It further states that —any aircraft or operation certificated by the FAA is subject to this surveillance regardless of whether they are operating as public or civil. Additionally, it states that —government-owned aircraft operators that are conducting public aircraft operations should be included in the FSDO's [Flight Standards District Office's] annual planned surveillance activities to ensure that the operator's status remains unchanged.

A search of FAA surveillance records of MSP Aviation Command revealed that, during the year before the accident, the FAA performed no surveillance inspections of MSP's flight

---

[57] In response to the increase in fatal accidents involving HEMS operations in 2008, the NTSB conducted a public hearing from February 3 through 6, 2009, to critically examine safety issues concerning this industry. Details of the hearing can be found on the NTSB's website at the following link: <http://www.ntsb.gov/events/hearing-hems/default.htm>.

operations. Specifically, there were no en route inspections, base inspections, station inspections, simulator inspections or checks, manual reviews, training program reviews, ramp inspections, or records inspections. Surveillance inspections of the MSP 14 CFR Part 145 maintenance repair station were routinely performed during the year prior to the accident.

In April 2009, MSP notified the FAA's Baltimore FSDO that it would like to seek 14 CFR Part 135 certification. On May 4, 2009, the commander of MSP Aviation Command discussed MSP's request with the manager of the Baltimore FSDO. According to the commander, the FSDO manager advised him that —the FAA now considers public helicopter operations ineligible for Part 135 certification; therefore, this new policy change precludes MSP Aviation Command from becoming Part 135 certified. The FSDO manager further advised the commander that he was awaiting further guidance on this issue from his superiors. In response to a request from the NTSB to explain why it considered MSP ineligible for Part 135 certification, the FAA provided a copy of a June 9, 2009, electronic mail message from the FSDO manager to other FAA personnel. In the message, the FSDO manager stated that he told the commander—that our Policy Divisions in FAA Headquarters were in the process of amending our guidance and that MSP Aviation Command may not be eligible to apply for or to hold a 135 Air Carrier Certificate. Additionally, the FAA provided a copy of a June 26, 2009, letter from the Associate Administrator for Aviation Safety to MSP, which stated, in part:

> The information from the Baltimore Flight Standards District Office (FSDO) that the Maryland State Police (MSP) Aviation Command was not eligible to hold a 14 CFR part 135 operating certificate may not be correct.

The letter also stated that MSP could begin the process of obtaining a Part 135 certificate by submitting a Preapplication

---

[58] FAA Order 8900.1 contains aviation safety policy used by aviation safety inspectors in performance of their official duties.

Statement of Intent to the Baltimore FSDO and suggested that MSP could, while waiting for the FAA to process its certificate request—immediately adopt, and comply with, the more stringent 14 CFR part 135 regulations required by the FAA for 14 CFR part 135 air carriers without having such a certificate.

CHAPTER 2

ADDITIONAL INFORMATION

Public versus Civil Aircraft Operations

EMS operations are conducted by both civil and public operators. Civil operators conduct these operations for hire under 14 CFR Part 135. Forty public operators currently provide air medical transportation using helicopters in the United States. 59 Unless such transportation results in compensation, these public operators are not required to hold an FAA air carrier certificate. 60

Public aircraft are exempt from many FAA regulations applicable to civil aircraft. However, Public Law 103-411, the Independent Safety Board Act Amendments of 1994, redefined —public aircraft. The statute, which became effective April 23, 1995, narrowed the definition of public aircraft with the intent that government-owned aircraft that operate for commercial purposes or engage in transport of passengers be subject to the regulations applicable to civil aircraft. In testimony supporting passage of the law, as recorded in the Congressional Record: October 3, 1994, Congressman Norman Mineta stated, in part:

It is intended to require, for the first time, that the Federal Aviation Administration regulations apply to aircraft operated by government entities. This requirement does not apply to certain governmental functions, such as firefighting, search and rescue, and law enforcement. Rather, it is intended to apply to all operations in which government officials or other individuals are transported on government-owned aircraft. It is expected that if public use aircraft are required to adhere to the Federal Aviation regulations, the safety of these operations will be enhanced.

Also, in the Congressional Record: October 6, 1994, in regard to the purpose of the law, Senator Larry Pressler stated, in part:

Its purpose is to advance the safety of travel on public aircraft; that is, aircraft used exclusively in the service of federal, state, and local governments. Under current law, public use aircraft are not subject to Federal Aviation Act safety regulations to the extent imposed on civil aircraft.

My provision would amend the definition of public use aircraft to mandate that FAA safety regulations, directives and orders issued for civil aircraft be made applicable to all government-owned, nonmilitary aircraft engaged in passenger transport.

Title 49 U.S.C. Section 40102(a)(16) states that —civil aircraft means an aircraft except a public aircraft. As defined in 49 U.S.C. Section 40102(a)(41)(C), a —public aircraft includes

An aircraft owned and operated by the government of a State, the District of Columbia, or a territory or possession of the United States or a political subdivision of one of these governments, except as provided in section 40125(b).

Title 49 U.S.C. Section 40125(b) states that an aircraft described in subparagraph (C) of Section 40102(a)(41) does not qualify as a public aircraft —when the aircraft is used for commercial

---

[59] NTSB staff determined this number by combining information provided by the Association of Air Medical Services, the Airborne Law Enforcement Association, and the Helicopter Association International.

[60] The NTSB is aware of one public operator—Lee County Division of Public Safety, Fort Myers, Florida—that holds a Part 135 air carrier certificate.

purposes or to carry an individual other than a crewmember or a qualified non-crewmember.

Title 49 U.S.C. Section 40125(a) defines —commercial purposes as —the transportation of persons or property for compensation or hire. It defines a —qualified non-crewmember as —an individual, other than a member of the crew, aboard an aircraft …whose presence is required to perform, or is associated with the performance of, a governmental function. A —governmental function is defined as —an activity undertaken by a government, such as national defense, intelligence missions, firefighting, search and rescue, law enforcement (including transport of prisoners, detainees, and illegal aliens), aeronautical research, or geological resource management.

According to FAA Advisory Circular (AC) 00-1.1, —Government Aircraft Operations, dated April 19, 1995, the status of an aircraft as a —public aircraft or —civil aircraft depends on its use in government service and the type of operation that the aircraft is conducting at the time. Government agencies may conduct both public and civil aircraft operations with the same aircraft. The AC states, —rather than speaking of particular aircraft as public aircraft or civil aircraft, it is more precise to speak of particular operations as public or civil. On the subject of—Medical Evacuation, the AC states:

> While this term is not considered synonymous with —search and rescue, it may be an included governmental function, depending on the particular circumstances of the operation. Again, the use of an aircraft must be essential to the successful performance of the mission. It is unlikely that the use of an aircraft would be essential for a medical evacuation operation in an urban area where other means of transportation are routinely available.

Regarding medevac flights, FAA Order 8900.1, Chapter 14 Public Aircraft, Section 1,—General Information on Public Aircraft Operations, dated September 13, 2007, states, in part:

The term —search and rescue does not include routine medical evacuation of persons due to traffic accidents and other similar incidents or hospital-to-hospital patient transfers.

The order further states:

Medical evacuation, as a general matter, is not considered a government function unless:

1. The nature of the operation requires the use of an aircraft with special configurations, which may not be eligible for a standard airworthiness certificate,

2. The victim cannot be accessed by ground transportation,

3. Insufficient number of properly certified and equipped civil aircraft operating under the appropriate rule, are available to complete the mission, or

4. Other, similar non-routine factors are present.

When the accident occurred, the MSP considered Aviation Command medevac flights to be civil aircraft operations. A memorandum from the commander addressed to all Aviation Command personnel on the subject of —Public Aircraft (Use) vs. Civil Aircraft (Part 91) Operations, dated March 5, 2008, was issued —to provide background information and to clarify our operational status as it relates to our mission profile and the airworthiness of our aircraft. After discussing Public Law 103-411 and the material in AC 00-1.1, the memorandum's conclusion section states, in part (underlining in the original):

> When Aviation Command pilots are involved in a flight operation that would be considered a —civil aircraft operation, i.e. medevac operations, VIP transports, training flights, mechanic transports, photo flights, etc.: we are operating under [Federal Aviation Regulations] part 91, as well as our policy and procedures outlined within the Command's Operations, Active Policies, and Standardization Manuals. When Aviation Command pilots are

involved in a flight operation that would be considered —public aircraft operation (and the mission meets the operational definition of same), i.e. search and rescue mission and law enforcement support/homeland security operations, etc.; we are operating within the standard operating procedures and standards outlined within the Aviation Command's Operations, Active Policies and Standardization Manuals for that particular operation. However, while Public Law 103-411 and AC 00-1.1 does allow government agencies to conduct both —civil —public aircraft operations with the same aircraft, operators of aircraft used for —dual purposes, as is the case with MSP Aviation Command, the government agencies are required to maintain the airworthiness of the aircraft in accordance with the appropriate regulations applicable to civil aircraft operations as outlined in [Federal Aviation Regulations P]art 43 and 91, as applicable.

On January 28, 2000, the FAA's regional counsel for the Great Lakes region, responded to a letter from Washington Hospital Center requesting an opinion regarding certain operations being conducted by MSP aircraft. In addressing the question of whether the interhospital air transfer of patients is a public or civil operation, the FAA's letter stated, in part:

The information you provided states that the Maryland State Police operates aircraft under [14 CFR] Part 91 of the Federal Aviation Regulations. This would seem to indicate that the aircraft and pilots meet the requirements for civil aircraft operation. Therefore, so long as the MSP does not receive compensation from the hospital or patients for the air transportation portion of the interhospital transfers, these flights may be conducted as civil aircraft operations under Part 91.

On December 3, 2008, NTSB investigators made a written request for the FAA to render its opinion on the public aircraft status of Trooper 2. A memorandum dated March 13, 2009, from FAA's Office of the Chief Counsel stated, —we believe the flight to have been a public aircraft operation within the meaning of the statute and FAA guidance material. The memorandum referenced the definition of public aircraft in 49 U.S.C. Section 40102(a)(41)(C) and the exception provided in 49 U.S.C. Section 40125(b). The memorandum stated, in part:

> The exception in section 40125(b) states that an aircraft does not qualify as public when it is used for commercial purposes or to carry an individual other than a crewmember or a qualified non-crewmember.
>
> The operation of Trooper 2 does not meet the exception as being used for commercial purposes. Our understanding is that the funding for the Maryland State Police helicopter operations is public, through fees and other taxes, and does not fall within the meaning of —for compensation or hire under the statute (section 40125(a)(1)). The recipients of the service provided by the Maryland State Police (in this case, the accident victims) do not pay for the service in any manner that could be construed as compensation or hire, and are considered —qualified non-crewmembers as they are individuals who are —associated with the performance of a governmental function. While the statute contains examples of governmental function, it does not specifically call out flights for medical evacuations. However, the FAA considers helicopter emergency medical services as akin to the—search and rescue function used as an example in the statute, and as falling within the statutory intent of governmental function.

Additionally, the memorandum stated that the FAA was —aware that internal agency materials may not be consistent in the consideration of the statutory factors or historical decisions and that these materials were being updated.

Protocols for Medevac Helicopter Request

Through its EMS Board, MIEMSS provided guidance to medical responders in Maryland for choosing between helicopter or ambulance transport. The guidance was given in the form of a trauma decision tree developed by the American College of Surgeons and adopted by the state of Maryland. This tree provided standards based on mortality and injury evidence for responders to classify four levels of serious injury consistent with required treatment at a trauma center, from—A—(the most serious) to —D (the least serious). The tree also provided guidance concerning when to use helicopter transport. For patients in categories A and B, it stated, —Consider helicopter transport if quicker or of clinical benefit. For patients in categories C and D, it stated,—Patients within a 30-minute drive time of the closest appropriate trauma/specialty center shall go by ground unless there are extenuating circumstances. Consider helicopter transport if of clinical benefit.

Responders to the automobile accident from the Waldorf fire station, who were among the first at the scene, confirmed that they were all familiar with the trauma decision tree and employed it in their evaluations of the accident victims. They had received training on recent upgrades to the trauma decision tree through a 60- to 90-minute video presented at their station house between January and May 2008, and their use of the tree was regularly reinforced at station safety reviews.

In the case of the automobile accident, paramedics classified the victims as category C [61] and decided they required treatment at a trauma center because of two factors: intrusion of the passenger compartment greater than 18 inches and patient complaints of back and neck pain. Helicopter transport was requested because the responders recognized that driving to the nearest trauma center, located at PGH, would take more than 30 minutes on wet and slippery roads. Based on a postcrash investigation, MIEMSS determined that the automobile accident site was a 48-minute drive from PGH and concluded that the decision to request helicopter transport to a trauma center was appropriate.

As a result of the helicopter accident, MIEMSS updated the trauma decision tree in the state of Maryland to require consultation with a local emergency room or trauma center for victims classified as C or D in order to reach agreement on the most appropriate mode of transport. According to the executive director of MIEMSS, the dispatch center (SYSCOM) has coordinated these consultations efficiently and there have been more joint decisions to use ground transportation. MIEMSS will evaluate mortality trends to judge the effectiveness of this new rule.

In addition to its internal postaccident review, MIEMSS and the Governor of Maryland convened an expert panel to conduct a review of the HEMS program operated in Maryland. 62 With regard to the physician consultation rule for Category C and D patients, the panel's November 2008 report stated, —it appears to be a prudent and reasonable approach to curtail air transport of more minor trauma patients. The panel reported that during the first 7 weeks after the protocol change, there was a marked reduction in HEMS usage in the state of Maryland. However, the panel pointed out that it was premature to judge the effect of this change on patient outcomes.

Further, in 2004, in response to increasing helicopter use, MIEMSS initiated development of a quality assurance procedure to assist local jurisdictions in evaluating the need for helicopter transports. Using satellite imagery, MIEMSS generated plots of each trauma center in the state with shaded zones around the trauma center representing areas within about 15 to 30 minutes driving time and dots to show the locations where medevacs to accident scenes had been performed. In 2007, these plots were shared with the local jurisdictions, and whenever helicopter transport had been requested from a shaded zone, MIEMSS asked the local jurisdiction to review the launch decision. According to the executive director of MIEMSS, the response from the local jurisdictions was positive, and requested helicopter launches have declined by about 23 percent since this program began. The executive director stated that he believed the use of satellite mapping for quality assurance, as well as

[61] The patients were initially classified as category D when the helicopter request was made.
[62] The Expert Panel Review of Helicopter Utilization and Protocols in Maryland can be found online at<http:// www. miemss.org/home/ Link Click. aspx? fileticket=Wc3WFoQSevY%3d&tabid=161&mid=569>.

the use of a consultation rule, might be useful for national standards and suggested a forum, which might be sponsored by the Office of Injury Control within the Centers for Disease Control and Prevention and by the National Highway Traffic Safety Administration, be held to review national standards on the use of aeromedical services in the transport of trauma victims.

Review of usage data obtained from MIEMSS shows a steady decline in the number of patients transported on MSP medevac flights each fiscal year (FY) from 2005 to 2008, followed by a marked reduction in FY 2009 (July 1, 2008 to June 30, 2009). (See table 2.) Between FY2005 and FY2008, there was a 19.7 percent reduction in the number of patients transported by MSP. Between FY2008 and FY2009, there was a reduction of 42.7 percent.

Table 3. Number of Patients Transported by MSP Aviation.

Year	Scene Medevacs	Percent Decline from Prior Year	Percent Decline from FY2005
FY2005	5,126 patients		
FY2006	4,874 patients	4.9%	4.9%
FY2007	4,634 patients	4.9%	9.6%
FY2008	4,114 patients	11.2%	19.7%
FY2009	2,356 patients	42.7%	54.0%

The NTSB recently issued a recommendation to the Department of Homeland Security's Federal Interagency Committee on Emergency Medical Services (FICEMS) [63] recommending that it develop national guidelines for the selection of appropriate emergency transportation modes for urgent care.

---

[63] FICEMS is an advisory committee whose function is to provide guidance and coordination on EMS. No federal agency is currently responsible for EMS oversight at the national level.

Previous Related Safety Recommendations

Safety of EMS Flights

On February 7, 2006, as a result of an NTSB special investigation of a number of accidents between January 2002 and January 2005 involving aircraft performing EMS operations, the NTSB issued four safety recommendations to the FAA addressing EMS operations. [64] On October 28, 2008, these recommendations were added to the NTSB's Most Wanted List of Safety Improvements.

Following are the recommendations and the FAA's responses:

A-06-12

Require all emergency medical services operators to comply with 14 Code of Federal Regulations Part 135 operations specifications during the conduct of all flights with medical personnel on board.

On January 23, 2009, the FAA published revised Operations Specification A021, which requires that all civil EMS flights with medical personnel on board, regardless of the presence of patients, be subject to the weather minimums limitation in 14 CFR Part 135. [65] Also on January 23, 2009, the NTSB responded that, although the revised operations specification is responsive to the recommendation, the FAA still needed to require the Part 135 flight and duty time limitations for EMS flights in order to fully meet the intent of the recommendation, and the NTSB classified Safety Recommendation A-06-12 —Open—Unacceptable Response.

---

[64] For more information, see Emergency Medical Services (EMS) Operations, Special Investigation Report NTSB/SIR-06-01 (Washington, DC: National Transportation Safety Board, 2006).

[65] Title 14 CFR Part 135.203(b) requires helicopters operating under VFR to maintain a minimum altitude of 300 feet agl over congested areas. Part 135.205(b) and Part 135.207 require a minimum visibility of 1 mile and visual surface light reference, respectively, to operate a helicopter at night.

A-06-13

Require all emergency medical system (EMS) operators to

develop and implement flight risk evaluation programs that include training all employees involved in the operation,

procedures that support the systematic evaluation of flight risks, and consultation with others trained in EMS flight operations if the risks reach a predefined level.

In August 2005, the FAA issued Notice N 8000.301, —Operational Risk Assessment Programs for Helicopter Emergency Medical Services, which provided detailed guidance on the development and use of flight risk evaluation plans by EMS operators. This notice expired in August 2006 without further FAA action for almost 2 years. In May 2008, the guidance within the expired notice was incorporated into FAA Order 8900.1, —Flight Standards Information Management Systems. On January 23, 2009, the NTSB informed the FAA that although guidance is valuable, Safety Recommendation A-06-13 asked for a requirement, such as an operations specification, that all EMS operators develop and use flight risk evaluation programs. Pending incorporation of a specific requirement to develop and use a flight risk assessment program, Safety Recommendation A-06-13 was classified —Open Unacceptable Response.

A-06-14

Require emergency medical services operators to use formalized dispatch and flight-following procedures that include up-to-date weather information and assistance in flight risk assessment decisions.

In May 2008, the FAA published AC 120-96, which provides detailed guidance about the creation and operation of operations control centers for helicopter EMS operations. On January 23, 2009, the NTSB indicated that, although the AC was responsive to the recommendation, it was only guidance, and that the FAA needed to require that all EMS operators incorporate the guidance contained in the AC into their operations. Pending that action, Safety Recommendation A-06-14 was classified —Open— Acceptable Response.

> A-06-15
>
> Require emergency medical services (EMS) operators to install terrain awareness and warning systems [TAWS] on their aircraft and to provide adequate training to ensure that flight crews are capable of using the systems to safely conduct EMS operations.

In June 2006, at the FAA's request, RTCA, Inc. [66] established a committee tasked with developing helicopter TAWS (H-TAWS) standards. In March 2008, the commission completed the development of minimum operational performance standards for H-TAWS. On December 17, 2008, the FAA published Technical Standards Order C194, —Helicopter Terrain Awareness and Warning System based on the commission standards. The FAA must now initiate rulemaking. On January 23, 2009, the NTSB indicated that the continuing delays in development of a final rule to require H-TAWS were not acceptable. Pending issuance of a final rule to mandate the installation and use of TAWS on all EMS flights, Safety Recommendation A-06-15 was classified —Open— Unacceptable Response.

Safety of Public HEMS Flights

On September 24, 2009, as a result of testimony given at the NTSB's public hearing on HEMS safety in February 2009 and the investigative findings of several 2008 HEMS accidents, the NTSB issued safety recommendations to the FAA, public HEMS operators, and other federal agencies. Following are the five recommendations made to public HEMS operators:

---

[66] RTCA, Inc. is a private, not-for-profit corporation that develops consensus-based recommendations regarding communications, navigation, surveillance, and air traffic management system issues.

A-09-97

Conduct scenario-based training, including the use of simulators and flight training devices, for helicopter emergency medical service (HEMS) pilots, to include inadvertent flight into instrument meteorological conditions and hazards unique to HEMS operations, and conduct this training frequently enough to ensure proficiency.

A-09-98

Implement a safety management system program that includes sound risk management practices.

A-09-99

Install flight data recording devices and establish a structured flight data monitoring program that incorporates routine reviews of all available sources of information to identify deviations from established norms and procedures and other potential safety issues.

A-09-100

Install night vision imaging systems in helicopters used for emergency medical services (HEMS) and require HEMS pilots be trained in their use during night operations.

A-09-101

Equip helicopters that are used in emergency medical services transportation with autopilots, and train pilots to use the autopilot if a second pilot is not available.

These recommendations are currently classified —Open—Await Response.

National Guidelines for Selection of Emergency Transportation Modes

In its September 24, 2009, letter to FICEMS, the NTSB stated that public hearing testimony indicated that a variety of standards are used by providers and organizations to determine when an EMS helicopter should be used to transport patients. No nationwide standards or recommended guidelines exist. Absent such criteria, the decision to undertake a HEMS flight may be made whether the medical situation merits the HEMS flight and its associated risks (compared to ground transportation) or not. Therefore, the NTSB issued Safety Recommendation A-09-103, which asked FICEMS to do the following:

> Develop national guidelines for the selection of appropriate emergency transportation modes for urgent care.

This recommendation is currently classified —Open—Await Response.‖

Flight Recorder Systems

The NTSB's first participation in a helicopter accident investigation in which an FDR was on board involved the August 10, 2005, accident of a Sikorsky S-76C+ helicopter that experienced an upset and crashed into the Baltic Sea, killing all 12 passengers and 2 pilots. [67] Importantly, without the FDR data, investigators would not have been able to identify the airworthiness issue that resulted in the issuance of three urgent safety recommendations by the NTSB on November 17, 2005 (Safety Recommendations A-05-33 through

---

[67] The Aircraft Accident Investigation Commission of Estonia investigated the accident with the assistance of accredited representatives from the NTSB and the Finland Accident Investigation Board under the provisions of Annex 13 to the International Convention on Civil Aviation.

-35). [68] The NTSB issued an additional recommendation, Safety Recommendation A-06-017, on March 7, 2006, asking the FAA to do the following:

> Require all rotorcraft operating under 14 Code of Federal Regulations Parts 91 and 135 with a transport-category certification to be equipped with a cockpit voice recorder (CVR) and a flight data recorder (FDR). For those transport-category rotorcraft manufactured before October 11, 1991, [69] require a CVR and an FDR or an onboard cockpit image recorder with the capability of recording cockpit audio, crew communications, and aircraft parametric data.

On May 22, 2006, the FAA informed the NTSB that it would review and identify changes in FDR technology since 1988 to ensure that current technology used in airplanes is appropriate for helicopter operations. The FAA stated that it would consider changes to its regulations based on this review. On November 29, 2006, the NTSB indicated that it did not believe the FAA's study was necessary and that it should begin the process to mandate that all rotorcraft operating under Parts 91 and 135 with a transport-category certification be equipped with a CVR and an FDR. Pending the FAA initiating such a requirement, Safety Recommendation A-06-17 was classified —Open —Unacceptable Response.

---

[68] Safety Recommendation A-05-33 asked the FAA to require Sikorsky S-76 helicopter operators to 1) conduct an immediate internal leakage test of all main rotor actuators with more than 500 hours since new and/or overhaul; 2) conduct subsequent recurrent tests at a period not to exceed 500 hours; 3) report the test results to the FAA and/or Sikorsky; and 4) correct any problems as necessary. This recommendation is classified —Open—Acceptable Action. Safety Recommendation A-05-34 asked the FAA to require Sikorsky S-76 helicopter operators to 1) conduct immediate visual and laboratory examination of hydraulic fluid and filter elements in hydraulic systems with actuators with more than 500 hours since new and/or overhaul for plasma flakes or other contamination that exceeds the manufacturers' allowable limits of concentration and size; 2) conduct subsequent recurring tests at a period not to exceed 500 hours; 3) report findings of contamination and flakes to the FAA and/or Sikorsky and 4) correct any problems as necessary. This recommendation is classified —Open—Acceptable Action.

Following its investigation of a July 27, 2007, accident involving two electronic newsgathering helicopters that collided in midair while maneuvering in Phoenix, Arizona, [70] neither of which was equipped with an FDR, the NTSB issued Safety Recommendation A-09-11 on February 9, 2009, which asked the FAA to do the following:

> Require all existing turbine-powered, non-experimental, non-restricted-category aircraft that are not equipped with a flight data recorder and are operating under 14 Code of Federal Regulations Parts 91, 121, or 135 to be retrofitted with a crash-resistant flight recorder system. The crash-resistant flight recorder system should record cockpit audio (if a cockpit voice recorder is not installed), a view of the cockpit environment to include as much of the outside view as possible, and parametric data per aircraft and system installation, all to be specified in European Organization for Civil Aviation Equipment document ED-155, Minimum Operational Performance Specification for Lightweight Flight Recorder Systems, when the document is finalized and issued.

In August 2009, European Organization for Civil Aviation Equipment document ED-155 was approved and published. On August 27, 2009, pending the FAA's issuance of a technical standards order that includes the specifications of ED-155, Safety Recommendation A-09-11 was classified —Open—Acceptable Response.

---

[69] Several sections of the regulations were changed on October 11, 1991, to upgrade the flight recorder requirements to require that multiengine, turbine-engine powered airplanes or rotorcraft having a passenger seating configuration, excluding any required crewmember seat, of 10 to 19 seats be equipped with a digital flight recorder.

[70] For more information, see Midair Collision of Electronic News Gathering Helicopters KTVK-TV, Eurocopter AS350B2, N613TV, and U.S. Helicopters, Inc., Eurocopter AS350B2, N215TV Phoenix, Arizona, July 27, 2007, Aviation Accident Report NTSB/AAR-09-02 (Washington, DC: National Transportation Safety Board, 2009).

Obstructive Sleep Apnea

On August 7, 2009, the NTSB issued three recommendations to the FAA about the need to educate, screen, and treat pilots for obstructive sleep apnea, a medically treatable sleep disorder in which an individual's airway is repeatedly blocked during sleep, resulting in daytime decrements in alertness and cognitive functioning. Specifically, the NTSB recommended that the FAA do the following:

> Modify the Application for Airman Medical Certificate to elicit specific information about any previous diagnosis of obstructive sleep apnea and about the presence of specific risk factors for that disorder. (A-09-61)

> Implement a program to identify pilots at high risk for obstructive sleep apnea and require that those pilots provide evidence through the medical certification process of having been appropriately evaluated and, if treatment is needed, effectively treated for that disorder before being granted unrestricted medical certification. (A-09-62)

> Develop and disseminate guidance for pilots, employers, and physicians regarding the identification and treatment of individuals at high risk of obstructive sleep apnea, emphasizing that pilots who have obstructive sleep apnea that is effectively treated are routinely approved for continued medical certification. (A-09-63)

These recommendations are currently classified —Open—Await Response.

Minimum Safe Altitude Warning

FAA radar systems are capable of providing minimum safe altitude warning (MSAW) service to aircraft under ATC control. The service is normally provided only to aircraft operating on an IFR transponder code.

Trooper 2 was operating on a transponder code that was pre-assigned to the MSP helicopter at ADW. This code was classified by the PCT radar processing system as a VFR code, which was ineligible for MSAW processing. However, before Trooper 2 received clearance for an IFR approach, a new code that would make the aircraft eligible for MSAW service should have been issued by the PCT controller but was not.

The FAA was asked by NTSB investigators to determine whether Trooper 2's flightpath would have caused an MSAW alert had the helicopter been on an MSAW-eligible code. The FAA's MSAW performance analysis determined that no MSAW alerts would have been issued for Trooper 2.

CHAPTER 3

ANALYSIS

General

The pilot was properly certificated and qualified in accordance with MSP standards. Additionally, although the FAA classified the flight as a public operation, the pilot was qualified under 14 CFR Part 91 to conduct the flight under VFR or IFR as a civil operation.

The helicopter was properly certificated, equipped, and maintained in accordance with the requirements in 14 CFR Parts 43 and 91 applicable to civil aircraft operating under VFR or IFR. The recovered components showed no evidence of any preimpact structural, engine, or system failures.

IMC prevailed in the accident area with scattered clouds near 200 feet agl and cloud ceilings near 500 feet agl. Although ADW was reporting visibility of 4 miles in mist, lower visibilities in fog occurred locally in the accident area.

This analysis will address the following issues: risk assessments, pilot performance and training, TAWS, ATC deficiencies, SYSCOM duty officer performance, and emergency response. Patient transport decisions, flight recorder requirements, and oversight are also discussed.

Pilot's Decision to Accept the Flight

At the beginning of his shift, the pilot obtained a computerized weather briefing from the FAA's DUAT service. Although the briefing the pilot obtained included observations, forecasts, and other information, it did not include weather hazards, a topic the pilot chose not to include in the briefing. If the pilot had included weather hazards, the briefing would have contained an AIRMET for IFR conditions issued at 1645 and valid until 2300 for an area that began immediately north and east of ADW, covered eastern Maryland and Delaware, and extended through New England. PGH was located within the boundaries of the AIRMET; ADW and the landing zone at Waldorf were not.

At the time of the briefing, the current weather at ADW indicated VFR conditions with a temperature/dew point spread of 1° C. The ADW forecast weather until 0100 on September 28 indicated VFR conditions, and between 0100 and 0200, the weather at ADW was expected to deteriorate to IFR conditions with the ceiling broken at 500 feet and overcast at 1,000 feet. The DCA forecast indicated that by 2200, the weather conditions were expected to deteriorate to IFR conditions with scattered clouds at 400 feet and ceiling overcast at 800 feet. These conditions were above the MSP Aviation Command minimums for acceptance of a night medevac flight (800 foot ceiling, 3 miles visibility). However, the ADW and DCA forecasts of deteriorating weather and the small temperature/dew point spread at ADW should have alerted the pilot to the possibility of local fog or low cloud formation as the evening progressed. According to FAA AC 00-6A, —Aviation Weather, pilots should anticipate fog when the temperature-dew point spread is 5° F (3.6° C) or less and decreasing.

Since the weather conditions were close to MSP minimums and the forecast called for conditions to deteriorate, the section was accepting flights on a —call by call basis, and MSP procedures required the pilot to conduct a check of the weather every 2 hours. The procedures did not specify what weather sources were considered acceptable for use in obtaining the required weather updates. There is no record of the pilot receiving another weather briefing during his shift either on the computer from DUAT or by calling a weather briefer. However, there is evidence that the pilot used the HEMS weather tool to check the weather before accepting the flight. Another pilot observed the HEMS weather tool displayed on the hangar computer after the accident, and the accident pilot's remarks suggest he was viewing the weather observations available through the tool during his conversation with the SYSCOM DO when he received the call for the flight. Normally, the surface weather observations for ADW, DCA, Fort Belvoir, and College Park are available through the HEMS weather tool. However, the weather reports for ADW and Fort Belvoir were not available on the night of the accident because of a technical failure of a DoD communications system. Therefore, the pilot was unaware that Fort Belvoir was reporting IFR conditions with a visibility of 1 1/4 miles in mist and a 0° temperature/dew point spread. It is unknown whether the pilot obtained the ADW weather (which was VFR conditions with a temperature/dew point spread of 0°) from another source, such as the airport's automatic terminal information service. [71]

During his conversation with the DO, the pilot specifically mentioned only the weather conditions at College Park and DCA. The weather reports for both of these locations met the MSP criteria for acceptance of a night medevac flight. However, College Park was at the 800-foot minimum ceiling for acceptance of a flight and was reporting a 0° temperature/dew point spread. The pilot's conversation with the DO indicated that the pilot was hesitant to accept the flight, as he was unsure he could make it to PGH due to deteriorating weather conditions. During the conversation, he stated

---

[71] Local (on airport) dissemination of the ADW observations was not affected by the DoD data communications failure.

that —maybe [the first responders] would change their mind about the flight request, indicating his reluctance to accept the flight. However, despite his misgivings, the pilot decided to accept the flight. The pilot's comments, —if they can do it we can do it, followed by, —yeah we ought to be able to do it…we're going to try it, show that his decision-making was influenced by the report that another medevac helicopter had just successfully completed a flight. This could have led the pilot to conclude the weather was better than reported.

Regardless of the unavailability of the DoD surface weather observations, the pilot did have access to information that indicated the weather conditions were continuing to deteriorate throughout the evening. In addition to surface observations, the pilot could also have viewed terminal area forecasts and AIRMETs via the HEMS weather tool. He could have obtained the amended terminal forecast for DCA, issued at 1933, which indicated that weather conditions were expected to deteriorate temporarily from VFR to IFR between 2000 and 2300 with the ceiling broken at 800 feet, overcast at 1,500 feet. Additionally, he could have obtained an AIRMET for IFR conditions issued at 2245 for an area that encompassed the entire route of Trooper 2. The forecast ceilings and visibilities in the DCA terminal forecast and in the AIRMET were above the MSP Aviation Command minimums for acceptance of a night medevac flight. However, the amendment to the DCA forecast and the issuance of the AIRMET indicated that weather conditions were continuing to deteriorate. Since HEMS weather tool data is not archived, it is not possible to determine what information was viewed by the pilot.

It appears that the pilot based his decision to launch solely on the weather observations at College Park and DCA and the suitable conditions implied by the other medevac helicopter's completed flight. Other pertinent weather data—the low temperature/dew point spreads at ADW and College Park, the AIRMET for IFR conditions encompassing the route of flight, and the continuing deterioration of the weather conditions as the evening progressed—were either discounted by the pilot or not obtained. If the pilot had thoroughly obtained and reviewed all of the available weather information, it is likely he would have realized that there was a high probability of encountering weather conditions less than MSP minimums on the flight and this would have prompted him to decline the flight. Therefore, the NTSB concludes that the pilot's decision to accept the flight, after his inadequate assessment of the weather, contributed to the accident.

According to the safety officer, at the time of the accident, MSP did not have a formal risk management program in place. He explained that there was optional guidance available to pilots in the form of a —Risk Assessment Matrix. However, review of the MSP Operations Manual revealed that it stated the flight crew —will apply the matrix and based on the risk assessment, increase visibility and ceiling minimums —to the crew's comfort level prior to accepting the mission. The matrix indicated that a temperature/dew point spread of less than 2° C raised the flight risk from low to medium risk. Although the matrix indicated that no flights were to be made if the risk level was high, it provided no instructions concerning medium-risk flights. There is no evidence indicating that the accident pilot consulted the matrix before the flight. Even if he had referred to it, the pilot might not have changed his decision to accept the flight, since the matrix did not provide clear guidance on medium-risk flights.

The NTSB notes that following the accident, MSP designed a new mission-specific flight risk assessment tool, and pilots are now required to use this tool before all flights. In addition to classifying the risk level as green (low), yellow (medium), or high (red), the new tool calculates a percentage associated with the operational risk. High-risk flights now require approval from the director of flight operations or a designee before a flight can be accepted. When medium-risk flights fall near the high end of the yellow range, the flight crew informs SYSCOM that any change in flight, such as deteriorating weather, could put them into the red and approval would be required to continue the flight or that the flight could be cancelled. Moreover, SYSCOM notifies the requesting agency that the estimated arrival time could be increased or the flight cancelled if there is an increase in operational risk. If this program had been in place at the time of the accident, then, when the pilot completed the risk assessment, he would likely have determined that the risk level was near the high end of the medium-risk range, which would have triggered the procedures described above, and the ensuing discussion may have resulted in cancellation of the flight. Therefore, the NTSB concludes that had a formal flight risk evaluation program been in place at MSP before the accident, it may have resulted in the cancellation of the flight.

Safety Recommendation A-06-13 asked the FAA to require all EMS operators to develop and implement flight risk evaluation programs. The FAA has provided guidance on the development and use of flight risk evaluation programs by EMS operators but has not required that all EMS operators implement flight risk evaluation programs. As a result, Safety Recommendation A-06-13 was classified —Open—Unacceptable Response. The NTSB believes that this accident demonstrates the need for all EMS operators, both public and civil, to develop and implement flight risk evaluation programs. Since the FAA does not have the authority to regulate public operators, even if the FAA were to require flight risk evaluation programs for HEMS operators, public operators would not be required to comply. Therefore, the NTSB recommends that all public HEMS operators develop and implement flight risk evaluation programs that include training for all employees involved in the operation, procedures that support the systematic evaluation of flight risks, and consultation with others trained in HEMS flight operations if the risks reach a predefined level.

Additionally, the NTSB continues to believe that the FAA should require all EMS operators to develop and implement flight risk evaluation programs that include training for all employees involved in the operation, procedures that support the systematic evaluation of flight risks, and consultation with others trained in EMS flight operations if the risks reach a predefined level. Therefore, the NTSB reiterates Safety Recommendation A-06-13.

Following the accident, MSP developed new procedures that involve the DO in flight risk assessment decisions. Before the accident, when a flight request was received, the DO passed the request directly to the flight crew. Under the new procedures, the DO evaluates the local and regional weather conditions displayed on the HEMS weather tool and can make a no-go decision based on this evaluation before the flight crew is notified. Also, as discussed previously, the DO is notified by the flight crew if the crew determines that the flight risk is near the high end of the yellow range, and the DO is then responsible for notifying the requesting agency that the helicopter's arrival could be delayed or the flight cancelled if the operational risk increases.

Safety Recommendation A-06-14 asked the FAA to require all EMS operators to use formalized dispatch and flight-following procedures (through ADS-B tracking) that include up-to-date weather information and assistance in flight risk assessment decisions. The FAA has published detailed guidance about the creation and operation of operations control centers for helicopter EMS operations, and, pending FAA action to require that all civil EMS operators follow the guidance, the NTSB classified Safety Recommendation A-06-14 as —Open— Acceptable Response. The NTSB notes that MSP does have formalized dispatch and flight following procedures, which are functions of SYSCOM, and that the SYSCOM DO has access to the HEMS weather tool, which provides up-to-date weather information. The NTSB further notes that the postaccident changes made by the MSP which involve the DO in flight risk assessment decisions are in accord with Safety Recommendation A-06-14. However, the NTSB is concerned that other public HEMS operators may not have operations control centers like SYSCOM that provide dispatch and flight-following service, weather information, and assistance in flight risk assessment decisions. Therefore, the NTSB recommends that that all public HEMS operators use formalized dispatch and flight-following procedures that include up-to-date weather information and assistance in flight risk assessment decisions.

Accident Sequence

The NTSB concludes that when the pilot was unable to reach PGH due to deteriorating weather conditions, he appropriately made the decision to divert to ADW and request ground transport for the patients. *Excellant !*

When the pilot contacted ADW tower, he reported to the controller that he was —on the localizer for runway 19R. At this time, the helicopter was about 6 nautical miles from the runway and tracking the localizer course at an altitude of 1,900 feet msl. Review of radar and ADS-B data showed that the helicopter's heading, turns, and intercept of the localizer course were smooth, uniform, and precise, consistent with autopilot use. Approximately 1 minute and 20 seconds after his initial call to ADW tower, the pilot reported that he was —not picking up the glideslope. The controller responded that her ILS equipment status display was indicating no anomalies with the equipment.

Radar and ADS-B data indicated that at the time of the pilot's transmission, the helicopter was maintaining a descent consistent with following the glideslope. (See figure 7 below.) Additionally, a postaccident flight test conducted by the FAA revealed no anomalies with the instrument approach equipment, and NTSB testing of the helicopter's navigation equipment found no deficiencies that would have precluded the pilot from capturing the glideslope. The NTSB was unable to determine which navigational frequencies the pilot had selected or what the pilot was seeing on his instruments. Thus, the NTSB concludes that no evidence was found that suggests that the glideslope was not functioning properly. Further, the lack of information regarding the accident airplane's navigation frequency settings and flight instrument indications precluded NTSB investigators from determining why the pilot believed he was not receiving a valid glideslope signal.

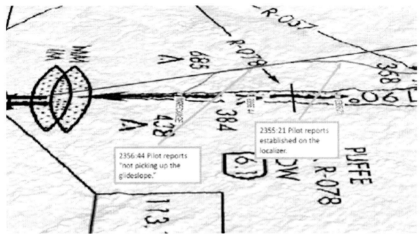

Figure 7. Comparison of Trooper 2's flightpath to the runway 19R glideslope. (Not to scale.) Blue line indicates runway 19R glideslope centerline; red line indicates Trooper 2's flightpath.

Even if the glideslope had failed, the accident pilot could *Follow Procedure* have continued the approach, following the localizer-only guidance and assuring terrain clearance by remaining at or above the localizer-only MDA of 680 feet msl. However, the pilot reque sted an ASR approach, which the controller stated that she was unable to provide because of her lack of currency on the procedure. *UNSAT!*

NTSB investigators considered two possible reason s for the pilot's request for a surveillance approach. One possibility was that the pilot did not have the ILS/LOC runway 19R approach chart visible as he was executing the approach to ADW. Therefore, he would not have been able to reference it to determine the MDA, the missed approach point, and other details of the localizer approach. Under this circumstance, the pilot's request for an ASR approach would be plausible because, if a surveillance radar approach had been provided, the controller would have advised the pilot that the MDA for the surveillance radar approach was 780 feet msl and instructed the pilot when to begin descent to the MDA. Additionally, at each mile of the final approach, the controller would have provided the pilot with the helicopter's distance from the missed approach point.

According to MSP Aviation Command personnel, the instrument approach charts were kept in a pouch on the right side of the pilot's seat and would have been readily accessible to the pilot. At the accident site, the charts were found scattered throughout the debris near the nose of the helicopter, precluding a determination of whether the pilot was looking at a particular chart while on approach to ADW.

Another possible reason for the pilot's request for an ASR approach was that he did not have the DME transceiver set to the frequency of the ADW VORTAC. The localizer approach to runway 19R requires DME readings off the ADW VORTAC to determine the final approach fix where descent to the MDA begins) and the missed approach point (where the pilot has to decide whether to continue to land or to abort the approach). As described in section earlier, the DME transceiver and the navigational receiver are usually set to the same frequency. Thus, in order to switch to the localizer frequency for runway 19R and retain DME information from the ADW VORTAC, the pilot would have had to select the —HOLD function on the navigation control head before switching frequencies. If the pilot did not select —HOLD before switching frequencies, the DME transceiver would have also been switched. The pilot would not have had any DME information and, therefore, would have had no means of determining the final approach fix or the missed approach point. Under this circumstance, the pilot's request for an ASR would again be plausible.

There was insufficient information available to determine whether either of these two scenarios was the reason that the pilot requested an ASR approach. Regardless of the reason for his request, once the controller denied it, the pilot still had many options available to conduct a safe landing in instrument conditions. He could have declared an emergency, which would have prompted the ADW controller to provide assistance, possibly including the ASR approach. Also, he could have executed a missed approach and attempted the ILS approach a second time to determine if the glideslope failure was a perceived failure or a legitimate one.

Don't be afraid to declare an emergency

Additionally, there were 11 other instrument approaches at ADW, any of which he could have requested.

About 27 seconds after the controller stated that she was unable to provide an ASR approach, upon reaching an altitude of about 1,450 feet msl on the glideslope and at a distance of about 4.0 miles north of the runway threshold, the helicopter's rate of descent increased rapidly from about 500 feet per minute (fpm) to greater than 2,000 fpm. The helicopter continued the descent, passing through the MDA for the localizer approach (407 feet agl), the alert height set on the radar altimeter (300 feet agl), and the decision height for the ILS approach (200 feet agl), before impacting trees and terrain about 3.2 miles north of the runway threshold. Data recovered from the PAR computer indicate that the helicopter impacted with the engines near idle power, the main rotor system at 100 percent rpm, and an indicated airspeed of about 92 knots. No evidence was found to indicate that the pilot made any attempt to arrest the helicopter's descent before impact.

The sudden increase in the helicopter's rate of descent may indicate that the pilot deliberately deviated from the approach procedure by attempting to —duck under the cloud layer to regain visual conditions. Several factors might have encouraged the pilot to attempt to —duck under the cloud ceiling. First, the outdated ADW weather report provided by the PCT controller indicated a ceiling of 1,800 feet and 7 miles visibility. Given these conditions, the pilot would have had a reasonable expectation that he could have descended below the cloud ceiling at an altitude well above the MDA for the approach.

Second, the pilot was based at ADW and familiar with its visual environment. This likely would have given him confidence that he would be able to identify landmarks and quickly determine his position once he descended below the cloud ceiling.

Third, a return to visual conditions would have relieved the pilot of the additional workload generated by instrument flight. All medical flights involve significant workload and time pressure to provide patients with timely service to medical aid. However, this flight involved unusually high workload once the pilot encountered instrument conditions. These conditions greatly increased the demands on the pilot since he had little recent experience in actual instrument flying. Additionally, the weather prevented him from reaching the planned medical center, forcing him to divert with the new responsibility of considering alternate transport arrangements for the patients along with his diversion considerations. Workload was further increased by the limited support he received from ATC, which included unresponsiveness, inefficient clearances to ADW, and an inability to provide a requested ASR approach. The NTSB therefore concludes that the pilot's workload increased substantially and unexpectedly as a result of encountering instrument weather conditions.

Further, the NTSB concludes that the pilot's expectation that he could descend below the cloud ceiling at an altitude above the MDA for the approach, his familiarity with ADW, and the reduction in workload a return to visual conditions would have provided are all factors that may have encouraged the pilot to deviate below the glideslope and attempt to —duck under the cloud ceiling. Fly the aircraft!

Regardless of the pilot's expectations for reaching VMC, once he deviated below the glideslope, he should have been prepared to level off at the MDA prescribed by the instrument approach procedure until he was able to confirm the airport environment as required by federal regulations. The pilot's failure to stop or slow the descent indicates that he was not aware of the helicopter's excessive descent rate or its height above the terrain, likely because he was looking outside the cockpit for the ground. At night, with low cloud ceilings, reduced visibility, and no surface light references, there were insufficient visual cues available for the pilot to establish ground reference.

The helicopter was equipped with a radar altimeter, which should have alerted the pilot when he descended below 300 feet agl, about 6 seconds before impact with the trees. [72] However, there was no decrease in the helicopter's descent rate after it passed through 300 feet agl. Testing of the radar altimeter revealed no discrepancies that would have prevented it from functioning normally during the accident flight. The NTSB concludes that the pilot failed to adhere to instrument approach procedures when he did not arrest the helicopter's descent at the MDA. The NTSB further concludes that although descent rate and altitude information were readily available through cockpit instruments, the pilot failed to monitor the instruments likely because he was preoccupied with looking for the ground, which he could not identify before impact due to the lack of external visual cues.

Additionally, NTSB investigators asked a manufacturer of TAWS to determine what pilot alerts would be expected if the helicopter had been equipped with TAWS. The manufacturer ascertained that three aural terrain alerts would have been generated at 7, 4, and 2 seconds prior to tree impact, and an aural glideslope alert would have been generated 24 seconds prior to tree impact if a valid glideslope signal was being received. It is unlikely the glideslope warning would have caused the pilot to arrest his descent since it appears that he intentionally deviated from the glideslope. However, if the helicopter had been equipped with a TAWS, the aural terrain alerts of —Caution Terrain,—Warning Terrain, and —Pull-up, would have been provided. These would have been more salient than the alert provided by the radar altimeter and likely would have caused the pilot to attempt to arrest his descent. Although it is unknown whether the pilot could have recovered in time to avoid hitting the trees, this scenario does illustrate the potential benefit of TAWS.

---

[72] The 6-second duration was determined by converting the radar altimeter alert height of 300 feet agl to msl by adding the accident site elevation of about 200 feet, resulting in 500 feet msl and noting that the ADS-B target data indicate the helicopter descended through 500 feet msl about 6 seconds before the end of the data.

Safety Recommendation A-06-15 asked the FAA to require EMS operators to install TAWS on their aircraft. The FAA has not yet issued a rule to mandate the installation and use of TAWS on EMS flights, and as a result, on January 23, 2009, Safety Recommendation A-06-15 as classified —Open—Unacceptable Response. The NTSB believes that this accident demonstrates the need for all EMS operators, both public and civil, to equip their aircraft with TAWS. Therefore, the NTSB reiterates Safety Recommendation A-06-15. However, since the FAA does not have the authority to regulate public operators, even if the FAA were to require TAWS for EMS operators, public operators would not be required to comply. Therefore, the NTSB recommends that all public HEMS operators install TAWS on their aircraft and provide adequate training to ensure that flight crews are capable of using the systems to safely conduct HEMS operations.

Air Traffic Control

On Trooper 2's initial contact with PCT, the pilot stated that he was climbing to 2,000 feet and requested an approach to ADW. Although the PCT controller acknowledged Trooper 2's initial contact, after the pilot stated his request, the controller did not respond for over a minute. The pilot called again, and the controller responded with an instruction to contact DCA tower, completely disregarding the pilot's request for an approach to ADW. The pilot had to restate his request before the controller began to handle the flight as an ADW arrival.

While Trooper 2 was being vectored for the approach, the controller stated that the current ADW weather was 1,800 broken, visibility 7 miles, temperature 21 °C, and dew point 19 °C. Review of ADW weather data showed that the weather given to the pilot had been issued at 1855 local time, almost 5 hours earlier. Weather information available to controllers is time-stamped, and the controller should have noticed that the report was outdated. The controller did not appear to have noticed the time discrepancy and did not advise the pilot of the age of the report or take any action to contact ADW for current weather information. During the time that the aircraft was being vectored for the approach, ADW was reporting wind from 110° at 3 knots, visibility 7 miles, cloud ceiling 1,300 broken, temperature 20° C, dew point 20 °C. Although these weather conditions were well above the localizer-only and ILS landing minimums for the runway 19R approaches, the cloud ceiling was 500 feet lower than that reported to Trooper 2. If the pilot had been given the current weather information, he would have expected to be unable to see the ground until he had reached a significantly lower altitude. Knowing that the ceiling was 500 feet lower may have discouraged the pilot from attempting to duck under the cloud ceiling and resulted in his continuing the approach to the airport at a 500 fpm rate of descent. Therefore, the NTSB concludes that the failure of the PCT controller to provide the current ADW weather information likely led the pilot to expect that he could descend below the cloud ceiling and establish visual contact with the ground at an altitude well above the MDA for the approach. *We are our best weather men Area Forecasts!*

The controller did not explicitly issue Trooper 2 an instrument clearance or an IFR transponder code. An IFR transponder code is necessary for aircraft to receive MSAW service. When interviewed, he stated that the pilot never requested an instrument clearance, and the controller believed that the pilot wanted a VFR practice approach to ADW. As the pilot had requested IFR from DCA and there was no further discussion of VFR operations by either the pilot or the PCT controller after he was handed off, the pilot could have reasonably expected that he was operating under IFR despite not having received an explicit IFR clearance from PCT. The controller's statement that he believed Trooper 2 was VFR all the way to touchdown is contravened by the controller's failure to restrict the aircraft to VFR operations as required by FAA directives. *WTF!* Between the time Trooper 2 contacted PCT and issuance of the IFR approach clearance, Trooper 2's status as an IFR or VFR flight was ambiguous. Once the helicopter was cleared for an approach without a VFR restriction, Trooper 2 was an IFR flight and should have been given an IFR transponder code.

Although the controller's failure to issue an IFR code resulted in Trooper 2 not being covered by MSAW service, postaccident MSAW analysis performed by the FAA and reviewed by NTSB determined that no MSAW alerts would have been issued for Trooper 2 even if the helicopter had been on an MSAW-eligible code.

Could it get any worse?

The PCT controller's handling of Trooper 2 as the aircraft approached the ILS localizer course was also deficient. The aircraft was turned to intercept the localizer late, resulting in an overshoot that was corrected by the pilot rather than the controller. The controller issued a heading of 170°, which would have allowed Trooper 2 to intercept the final approach course at an angle of about 20°, except that the instruction was issued too late. Trooper 2 crossed the localizer and had to turn to intercept the final approach course from the east side, requiring a heading of about 210°. The pilot corrected the poor intercept on his own, with no comment or assistance from the controller.

After Trooper 2 was transferred to ADW tower, the pilot reported that he was on the localizer and was cleared to land on the runway. Shortly afterward, Trooper 2 reported that he could not pick up the glideslope and requested an ASR approach. The ADW tower controller responded that she was not current to provide that service. As the pilot made no indication that he was in any difficulty, the controller's expectation was that Trooper 2 would complete a localizer approach. When interviewed, the controller stated that, if there had been any emergency need for the ASR approach, she would have provided it. However, this event raises the question of why she was not current. NTSB investigators found that lack of currency was widespread among ADW controllers and appears to have been the result of a lack of diligence on the part of ADW tower management in monitoring currency and ensuring that controllers remained qualified on all positions. Following the accident, about 75 percent of the controllers at ADW achieved currency on ASR approaches. Subsequently, the FAA suspended ASR approaches at ADW because of an internal dispute about

No surprise there

Privatization of ATC - IF Passed - how will effect ATC Quality?

whether the service would be provided by ADW or PCT. At the time of this writing, ADW ASR procedures remain suspended.

The NTSB concludes that air traffic services provided by the DCA and PCT controllers to the accident flight exhibited numerous procedural deficiencies, including unresponsiveness, inattention, and poor radar vectoring. These deficiencies were a distraction to the pilot and increased his workload by requiring him to compensate for the poor services provided.

Attention to detail!

Instrument Training and Experience

Prior to this accident, MSP had flown helicopters for 22 years without a fatal accident. The previous fatal accident, in 1986, involved an encounter with instrument conditions and subsequent collision with terrain. Following the 1986 accident, MSP emphasized the importance of instrument experience and proficiency among its pilots. The instrument training program remained the same until 10 months before the accident, when according to some pilots and instructors, the instrument training requirements were effectively downgraded.

Things that make you go hmmm . . . . .

Before the instrument training change in November 2007, MSP pilots performed six approaches every 6 months to maintain currency. The program was changed to require that pilots receive an IPC every 6 months. According to the chief pilot, he decided to change the training program because pilots were not conducting —quality training when practicing with other pilots. However, another instructor reported that the rationale behind the change was not just to have pilots fly with instructors but also to —save flight time by reducing the total flying time it took to remain qualified for the job.

Although pilots were still allowed to practice approaches in addition to the required IPCs, interviews revealed this was not happening. Interviews with pilots also revealed a concern that, although they were maintaining currency with the new training program, they were not maintaining proficiency. One instructor stated that he did not think two IPCs a year was enough training for pilots to maintain proficiency and that pilots needed to practice more than that. Another pilot stated that —getting half the previous number of practice approaches and going 6 months between training opportunities provides neither the frequency nor the quantity of instrument practice needed for this demanding and hazardous flying environment.

By definition, proficiency is a thorough competence derived from training and practice. Regarding instrument proficiency, an article by AOPA's Air Safety Foundation [73] states that instrument flying is a "use it or lose it" skill. The article suggests that in addition to FAA currency requirements, pilots have: a) at least 1 hour of simulated or actual instrument time in the previous month; b) at least one instrument approach in the same period; and c) an IPC in the previous 6 months. By following these suggestions for 1 year, a pilot should accumulate a minimum of 12 hours of instrument time, 12 instrument approaches, and 2 IPCs. TS low time acFT?

In the year prior to the MSP's change in its instrument training program, the pilot logged instrument time on 7 flights, accumulating 6.2 hours of instrument time, and completing 20 approaches. After the change and in the year prior to the accident, the pilot logged instrument time on only 2 flights, which included 2.1 hours of instrument time and 4 instrument approaches. This is a substantial reduction in training and well below that suggested by AOPA.

In addition to his limited instrument experience in the 12 months prior to the accident, the pilot had not flown at night under instrument conditions since October 29, 2006, 23 months before

---

[73] AOPA Air Safety Foundation is a nonprofit organization promoting safety and pilot proficiency in general aviation through training, education, research, analysis, and information dissemination. The referenced article, —Safety Hot Spot: Pilot Proficiency and the Flight Review, can be found online at<http://www.aopa.org/asf/hotspot/proficiency_check.html>.

Huh what?

the accident. Also, although the pilot had conducted the majority (20 out of 24) of his instrument approaches in the past 2 years at ADW, only 4 of those were non-precision approaches, and they did not include the localizer approach to runway 19R.

The NTSB concludes that although the pilot met the recent-experience requirements to act as PIC under IFR, he was not proficient in instrument flight. This lack of proficiency likely contributed to the pilot's failure to properly conduct what effectively became a non-precision approach at night in instrument conditions. Furthermore, the NTSB concludes that changes made by the MSP Aviation Command to its instrument training program about 10 months before the accident did not promote instrument proficiency. *- who's in charge of MSP Aviation? - who's in command?*

The NTSB notes that MSP Aviation Command has made postaccident changes in its training program including adding requirements for pilots to conduct —one instrument approach in VMC per month on the return leg of a missionland—one instrument approach flight per month with another check pilot. However, the NTSB is concerned that no requirements have been added for the performance of non-precision approaches or for the performance of instrument approaches at night. If the accident pilot had received more recent and targeted instrument training and had more opportunities to practice his instrument skills, he would have been better prepared to cope with the situation he encountered during the accident flight. This accident highlights the need for scenario-based training tailored to address the hazards unique to HEMS operations. The NTSB recently issued Safety Recommendation A-09-97 to all public HEMS operators, including MSP, recommending they conduct scenario-based training, including the use of simulators and flight training devices, for HEMS pilots, to include inadvertent flight into IMC and hazards unique to HEMS operations, and conduct this training frequently enough to ensure proficiency.

Has this happened? Rotor sim?
SIC proficiency?

Fatigue

The pilot was off duty for 2 days before the accident, and evidence indicates that his activities, behavior, and sleep schedule were routine. On the day of the accident, he awoke about 0800, conducted routine activities, and began the accident shift at 1900. There was no evidence available to determine if the pilot napped or drank coffee before he was notified about the accident mission at 2302, although both rest facilities and coffee were available and either would have benefited the pilot as a fatigue countermeasure.[74]

The accident occurred around the pilot's normal bedtime of midnight, about 16 hours after he had awakened from his nighttime sleep. Both the late hour and length of time awake are factors that could have produced fatigue. The accident pilot displayed two significant risk factors for obstructive sleep apnea: obesity and loud snoring.[75] The NTSB has recently issued recommendations to the FAA about a need to educate, screen, and treat pilots for obstructive sleep apnea, a medically treatable sleep disorder in which an individual's airway is repeatedly blocked during sleep resulting in daytime decrements in alertness and cognitive functioning. Such education, screening, and treatment may have benefitted the pilot, if he did suffer from a sleep disorder such as apnea. Untreated sleep disorders such as obstructive sleep apnea could have been an additional potential cause of fatigue for the accident pilot.

Police and air traffic recordings from the accident period revealed no gross deficiencies in alertness or pilot responsiveness (and in fact, as noted above, the pilot was sufficiently responsive to correct an air traffic controller's deficiencies in his handling).

---

[74] According to his wife, the pilot was normally able to nap during the day and regularly drank coffee.

[75] Medical literature suggests that loud snoring and obesity are significant risk factors for the presence of obstructive sleep apnea. See O. Resta, et. al. (2001). Sleep-related breathing disorders, loud snoring and excessive daytime sleepiness in obese subjects. International Journal of Obesity, 25, 669-675.

he was stressed!

However, the pilot made an improper decision to deviate from the published instrument approach procedure. Fatigue, in combination with the high workload the pilot was experiencing, could explain this uncharacteristically deficient decision. Therefore, based on the late hour, the length of time awake, the risk factors for sleep apnea exhibited by the pilot, and the decision to deviate from the published procedures, the NTSB concludes that the pilot was likely less than fully alert, and fatigue may have contributed to his deficient decision-making.

The NTSB recognizes that the implementation of a comprehensive program to educate, screen, and treat pilots of obstructive sleep apnea will take time. In the meantime, the NTSB recommends that the MSP implement a program to screen and—if necessary—treat its pilots for obstructive sleep apnea.

Survival Factors

As the helicopter descended into the trees, the forward right part of the airframe experienced a significant tree strike that immediately killed the pilot and tore away the right side of the fuselage, ejecting the secondary litter and patient, who survived. The helicopter then fell on its left side. The crash forces and reduction in volume of occupiable space within the cabin (resulting from both tree strikes and the secondary impact with the ground) precluded survival for the cabin occupants; and therefore, this accident is considered non-survivable. [76] Had the survivor remained inside the helicopter, she would likely have been fatally injured. Examination of the medic's restraints indicated they were not in use at the time of the accident. Given the loss of occupiable space within the cabin, it is unlikely that the medic's failure to restrain himself played a role in his death.

Miracles do happen! Praise God!

---

[76] For an accident to be deemed survivable, the forces transmitted to occupants through their seat and restraint system cannot exceed the limits of human tolerance to abrupt accelerations, and the structure in the occupants' immediate environment must remain substantially intact to the extent that a liveable volume is provided for the occupants throughout the crash.

SYSCOM

The SYSCOM DO made numerous errors on the night of the accident. In particular, he did not accomplish what MSP procedures specify as his primary duty: to ensure that all MSP Aviation Command helicopters were positively identified and tracked throughout each flight.

It is apparent that the DO lost situational awareness of the accident helicopter during the final minutes of the flight. The ADS-B trip history report indicated that the DO logged Trooper 2 as landed at ADW at 0002:02. At this time, he most likely also silenced the audible alarm associated with the loss of ADS-B tracking. When he received a call 16 minutes after the crash asking where Trooper 2 was, the DO immediately responded, —they landed at Andrews. When informed that ADW tower had lost Trooper 2 off radar, he was surprised. He then attempted to contact Trooper 2 by radio and got no response.

During the investigation, NTSB investigators learned that, against MSP operational policy, DOs routinely disregarded ADS-B loss of signal alerts and only attempted to contact flight crews when a signal was lost during cruise flight. This lack of adherence to policy created an institutional mindset that assumed that a helicopter had landed safely when its ADS-B signal was lost during the landing phase of flight. This problem was compounded because there was no requirement for flight crews to call back into SYSCOM within a specific timeframe after landing. The routine lack of positive feedback communication from helicopters allowed DOs to assume that aircraft had landed safely and, over time, safe landings were taken for granted.

The NTSB concludes that the MSP SYSCOM DO lost situational awareness of the helicopter while it was in flight. Further, the NTSB concludes that the lack of adherence to effective flight-tracking policies by MSP SYSCOM personnel created an institutional mindset that allowed DOs to assume that aircraft had landed safely when the ADS-B signal was lost; over time, safe landings were taken for granted.

In the memorandum detailing postaccident changes, the MSP indicated that it has resumed conducting unannounced, missing aircraft exercises. Additionally, flight crews are now required to call in to SYSCOM within 5 minutes of landing.

Emergency Response

Do what you got
to do

The wreckage was located by the pilot and medic of Trooper 8, who organized their own impromptu search effort. The two men took it upon themselves to travel by car to the search area after their air search had to be aborted due to weather conditions. After meeting with another MSP officer, they contacted ADW tower and, using the information obtained and their knowledge of aviation, correctly identified the most probable location of the accident and responded to Walker Mill Regional Park. The two men had been at Walker Mill Regional Park previously (after initially plotting the last known position coordinates they received from SYSCOM) but left the area after receiving information about a —ping from one of the troopers' cell phones.

At the time the two men located Trooper 2, both PG County and MSP search efforts were primarily focused on a construction area about 1.25 miles east of the accident site. This area was very expansive and dark and the process of obtaining sufficient four-wheel drive vehicles for a search would have taken considerable time. Additionally, visibility in the area was reported to be approximately 50 feet, which would have further slowed the search process. Given the darkness, fog, and delay in obtaining four-wheel drive vehicles, it would likely have taken several hours to thoroughly search the construction area. Until this area was searched, it is unlikely that Walker Mill Regional Park would have been searched. Therefore, the NTSB concludes that had two MSP aviation employees not pursued their own search effort, locating the accident site would likely have taken several more hours than it did.

Maryland State Police Search and Rescue

According to MSP operational policy at the time of the accident, the troopers at each barrack were to manage any incident that happened within their area of responsibility. Thus, the shift supervisor on duty at the Forestville barrack became the incident commander for the search until the barrack commander arrived about 0100 and took over. Both of these individuals were unfamiliar with aviation. The shift supervisor was not familiar with the flightpath inbound to ADW and was unable to tailor the search to the area directly along the flightpath. The barrack commander called MSP Forestville at 0154:39, almost 2 hours after the accident occurred, asking for Aviation Command units to respond to the command post at Forestville because, as she said, —we've got questions that we need them to answer about how things work. If these Forestville troopers had been more knowledgeable about aviation, it is likely that MSP resources could have been used more effectively in searching for the missing helicopter. The NTSB concludes that the incident commander's lack of aviation knowledge diminished the effectiveness of search and rescue activities. The NTSB recognizes that it is not feasible to provide aviation-specific training to every trooper in a barrack who might conceivably serve as an incident commander. Therefore, the NTSB recommends that the MSP revise its policy regarding incident commanders to specify that, in any event involving a missing or overdue aircraft, an Aviation Command trooper will serve as the incident commander.

About 0022:31, once he realized the helicopter was missing, the DO provided PG County dispatchers with Trooper 2's last ADS-B coordinates. He provided the coordinates by reading a string of numbers but did not mention the numbers were in the format of degrees, minutes, seconds. The PG County dispatchers assumed the coordinates were in the format of degrees, decimal degrees, which they were accustomed to using, and entered them in that format. The location returned by the software program was near Calvert Cliffs, Maryland, located about 30 miles southeast of the accident site. This location raised confusion among PG County personnel and, within 10 minutes, they called SYSCOM to verify the location. The PG County dispatcher reported the discrepancy to an operator at SYSCOM who responded, —okay I don't know where the duty officer got those [coordinates]....‖The operator did not communicate with the DO and verify the coordinates that were given to PG County dispatchers. Had the SYSCOM operator done so, the misunderstanding about the format of the coordinates might have been discovered, and the ongoing confusion about the helicopter being near Calvert Cliffs might not have persisted.

NTSB investigators found evidence indicating that MSP personnel outside SYSCOM were not familiar with latitude and longitude coordinates. Interviews with MSP personnel at the Forestville barrack clearly indicated a complete lack of knowledge, at the time of the accident, regarding latitude and longitude coordinates and how they could be used. MSP road troopers performed their daily duties by referencing ADC grid maps and were not aware that those maps contained latitude and longitude coordinates. Some MSP patrol cars were equipped with laptop computers and software that allowed users to enter latitude and longitude coordinates, but none of the troopers interviewed had received any training on how to use this function.

Therefore, the NTSB concludes that MSP troopers and SYSCOM personnel were insufficiently equipped and trained to conduct a search involving GPS coordinates, and that this hindered their ability to locate the site of the wreckage. In the memorandum detailing postaccident changes, the MSP indicated that it has provided instruction to all Aviation Command personnel and all MSP field personnel on the use and interpretation of latitude and longitude.

At the time of the accident, the software on the SYSCOM DO's console provided a view of the ADS-B data overlaid on an aviation sectional chart. There was no ability to overlay the data on other types of maps, such as a topographic map or a road map, which would have provided the DO with more information about

Trooper 2's last known position. For example, had the DO known that Trooper 2's last known position was in Walker Mill Regional Park, he would have provided this information to the incident commander at Forestville barrack, who would have undoubtedly sent more units to that location immediately. This would have obviated the need for MSP road troopers to know anything about GPS coordinates and given them a firm location with which to begin the search. It also would have ended the confusion about the helicopter being near Calvert Cliffs. MSP informed the NTSB that the software for ADS-B monitoring has been upgraded and is now capable of overlaying the data on ADC street maps, terrain maps, and satellite photos, as well as on aviation sectional charts.

<u>Prince George's County Search and Rescue</u>

During the search, PG County personnel offered to —ping the troopers' cell phones and possibly provide a better location to search. MSP accepted the offer and PG County personnel contacted the cellular service provider, who—pinged the cell phones and provided the street address of the closest cell phone tower. The cellular provider did not initially provide a distance or bearing from the tower to the cell phone, just the street address of the tower. Unfortunately, the street address location was immediately provided to PG County officers and MSP Forestville barrack troopers, and numerous officers responded to that location. Releasing the street address of the cell phone tower to all units without a distance and bearing only served to distract and confuse units that were already searching a more accurate location. (The SYSCOM DO had provided ADS-B coordinates of the helicopter's last known position.)

The NTSB concludes that neither PG County nor MSP dispatchers fully understood the importance of obtaining distance and bearing information, as well as the cell tower location, before releasing a location obtained from cell phone —pinging; this lack of understanding led dispatchers to provide a simple street address of the cell phone tower without context to all units involved in the search. This distracted and confused units already searching a more likely location. Therefore, the NTSB recommends that the MSP and PG County provide additional training to their dispatchers on the use of cell phone —pinging and include instruction about how to integrate the data obtained from cell phone pinging into an overall search and rescue plan.

FAA Search and Rescue Support

The ADW controller noticed that Trooper 2 was missing almost immediately after radar contact was lost, and she began attempting to contact the pilot. She also advised the ADW fire department chief, who was expecting to meet the helicopter, that Trooper 2 was out of contact. Although the controller's efforts did not follow the ADW tower emergency notification procedures precisely, all the emergency responders in the area were alerted within a few minutes of the accident either by the controller or by the ADW fire chief.

When asked, neither the ADW controller nor the PCT operations manager-on-duty was able to provide the coordinates of the helicopter's last known position. NTSB investigators determined that there were at least two ways that ADW or PCT could have provided the latitude and longitude of the location using ATC radar data. Postaccident discussions at PCT showed that a traffic management system known as "CountOps," which is available at both PCT and ADW, would have been able to provide a position of the last radar target within a few seconds. However, the ADW controller and the PCT operations manager were both insufficiently familiar with the system to use it for that purpose. Alternatively, recorded ATC radar data could have been used to establish the direction and distance from the ADW radar site of the last target for Trooper 2. Plotted on a map, the last radar target would have placed the helicopter in Walker Mill Regional Park. The NTSB concludes that the FAA ATC's inability to produce timely location data also hampered search and rescue efforts.

The NTSB concludes that knowledge of the disjointed search and rescue efforts and the techniques eventually employed to locate the accident site could provide valuable lessons to agencies, such as HEMS dispatch centers, 911 dispatch centers, and fire, police, and sheriff's departments, involved in search and rescue efforts. Therefore, the NTSB recommends that the National Association of Air Medical Communications Specialists, the Association of Public-Safety Communications Officials International, the National Emergency Number Association, the International Association of Police Chiefs, the National Sheriffs' Association, and the International Association of Fire Chiefs inform their members through their websites, newsletters, and conferences of the lessons learned from the emergency response to this accident, particularly emphasizing that search and rescue personnel need to understand how to interpret and use both GPS coordinates and the results of cell phone —pinging.

Other Related Issues

Today's BS calls?

Patient Transport Decisions

First responders to the automobile accident determined, using guidelines provided by MIEMSS, that the victims of the automobile accident required treatment at a trauma center. Per the guidelines, they requested helicopter transport, since the nearest trauma center, located at PGH, was more than a 30-minute drive from the accident site on wet and slippery roads. Following the accident, MIEMSS reviewed the first responders' decision and determined that the ambulance drive time would have been about 48 minutes. Therefore, MIEMSS concluded that first responders appropriately followed established guidelines on the scene of the auto accident when making the decision to request helicopter transport.

Although the NTSB does not dispute MIEMSS's conclusion that the guidelines in effect at the time were followed, the NTSB notes that, in this case and based on the radar data, if Trooper 2 had not been forced to divert to ADW by deteriorating weather conditions, it would have landed at PGH about 45 minutes after it was requested by the first responders. Compared to the ambulance drive time of about 48 minutes (the ambulance was already at the scene when Trooper 2 was requested), the use of a helicopter would have resulted in the patients arriving at the trauma center about 3 minutes faster.

Additionally, the NTSB notes that as a result of the helicopter accident, MIEMSS updated the guidelines to require that first responders caring for patients classified as Category C or D consult with a physician before HEMS transport is summoned. In this particular case, the victims were classified as Category C of the four level classification scheme, from —A (the most serious injury) to —D (the least serious injury), and under the revised guidelines, a consultation would have been required before Trooper 2 was requested. The report of the expert panel convened by MIEMSS to review Maryland's HEMS program stated that the new consultation rule —appears to be a prudent and reasonable approach to curtail air transport of more minor trauma patients—those rated as category C or D.

MIEMSS usage data show a notable decrease of 42.7 percent in the number of patients transported on MSP medevac flights from FY2008 (July 1, 2007, to June 30, 2008) to FY2009, which can be attributed to the implementation of the consultation rule. Testimony given at the NTSB public hearing on the safety of the HEMS industry indicated that providers and organizations use a variety of standards (of varying quality) to decide when to request helicopter transport. There are no nationwide standards or recommended guidelines. During the course of this investigation, the executive director of MIEMSS suggested that a forum should be held to develop national standards on the use of aeromedical services in the transport of trauma victims. The NTSB recently issued Safety Recommendation A-09-103 to FICEMS recommending that they develop national guidelines for the selection of appropriate emergency transportation modes for urgent care.

Consultation rule needs reviewed !

Special interest and Politics involved ?

Flight Recorder Systems

If a recorder system that captured cockpit audio, images, and parametric data had been installed on the accident helicopter, NTSB investigators would have been able to use the recorded data to determine additional information about the accident scenario, including navigation frequency settings and flight instrument indications. It is also possible that recorded images could have shown whether the pilot had the approach chart available to him. The NTSB concludes that having aboard the aircraft a recorder system that captured cockpit audio, images, and parametric data would have aided the NTSB in determining the circumstances that led to this accident.

The NTSB notes that the accident helicopter was not required to have a CVR or FDR installed. However, it would have been required to have either these devices or a cockpit image recorder if the FAA had implemented NTSB Safety Recommendation A-06-17. Safety Recommendation A-06-17 asked the FAA to require, among other things that transport-category rotorcraft manufactured before October 11, 1991, operating under 14 CFR Parts 91 and 135 be equipped with either a CVR and an FDR or a cockpit image recorder. The accident helicopter was a transport-category rotorcraft manufactured in 1988. When the NTSB issued this recommendation, it stated that transport-category helicopters should be equipped with flight recorders [77] in order to gather data critical to diagnosing shortcomings in the passenger-carrying helicopter fleet. Further, the NTSB stated that, although the FAA had increased the stringency of flight recorder requirements on passenger-carrying airplanes over a period of years, it had not universally applied these more stringent requirements to helicopters. On May 22, 2006, the FAA stated that it would review changes in FDR technology since 1988 and consider changes to its regulations based on this review. On November 29, 2006, the NTSB

---

[77] The term —flight recorders refers to all crash-protected devices installed on aircraft, including but not limited to, FDRs, CVRs, and onboard image recorders.

indicated that it did not believe the FAA's study was necessary and that it should begin the rulemaking process. As a result, Safety Recommendation A-06-17 was classified —Open—Unacceptable Response.

The NTSB continues to believe that the FAA should require all rotorcraft operating under 14 CFR Parts 91 and 135 with a transport-category certification to be equipped with a CVR and a FDR. For those transport-category rotorcraft manufactured before October 11, 1991, the FAA should require a CVR and an FDR or an onboard cockpit image recorder with the capability of recording cockpit audio, crew communications, and aircraft parametric data. Therefore, the NTSB reiterates Safety Recommendation A-06-17.

On February 9, 2009, the NTSB issued Safety Recommendation A-09-11 to the FAA, asking the FAA to require that all existing turbine-powered, non-experimental, non-restricted-category aircraft that are not equipped with an FDR and are operating under Parts 91, 121, or 135 be retrofitted with a crash-resistant flight recorder system. This recommendation is currently classified—Open—Acceptable Response. As a turbine-powered transport-category aircraft, the accident helicopter is covered by this recommendation. The NTSB notes that the accident that prompted issuance of Safety Recommendation A-09-11 involved a midair collision between two helicopters. This accident, which provides additional support for the recommendation, also involved a helicopter. These and other accidents demonstrate the need for flight recorders on helicopters as well as on airplanes.

Oversight

During the course of this investigation, the NTSB learned that the MSP has minimal oversight and surveillance by any outside organization. The Maryland state legislature oversees the MSP's budget but has no direct responsibility for the day-to-day operations of the MSP Aviation Command, nor do they have an aviation surveillance function similar to the FAA. [78] The FAA provides

What does budget look like today?
Cost effectiveness of T5?
W-139's? Funding?

oversight of MSP's aviation maintenance practices through its surveillance of MSP's 14 CFR Part 145 maintenance repair station but has not conducted any recent surveillance of MSP aviation operations.

FAA Order 8900.1 requires a nominal level of surveillance for public aircraft operators. The order states that government-owned aircraft operators conducting public aircraft operations should be included in the FSDO's annual planned surveillance activities to ensure that the operator's public status remains unchanged. Additionally, the order states that government-owned aircraft operators holding any type of FAA certification will be included in the normal surveillance activities, such as spot inspections (ramp checks) of the aircraft and aircraft records. Since MSP aircraft have airworthiness certificates, MSP should be included in normal surveillance activities. However, despite its own order requiring surveillance, the FAA had not conducted any recent operational surveillance of MSP. Even if the FAA had performed the minimal amount of surveillance currently required by Order 8900.1, it is unlikely this would have prevented the accident. However, if MSP had been operating under a 14 CFR Part 135 certificate, the FAA would have reviewed the changes MSP made to its instrument training program in November 2007 and may have required modification of the program to include conducting non-precision approaches, night approaches, and more frequent instrument practice. Additionally, the FAA would have reviewed MSP's operations manual and required the correction of any inconsistencies found between the manual and the procedures being followed. If the FAA had noted that the manual required the flight crew to apply the Risk Assessment Matrix before accepting each flight but that flight crews were not doing so, this may have resulted in the earlier implementation of a formalized flight risk management program at MSP. These types of changes may have prevented the accident.

The NTSB recently learned that MSP had informed the FAA's Baltimore FSDO that it wanted to seek 14 CFR Part 135 certification, and, although the initial verbal response the MSP received from the FSDO manager was not supportive, later written guidance from the FAA associate administrator for aviation safety encouraged MSP to proceed with the application process for Part 135 certification. Additionally, the associate administrator informed MSP that it could —immediately adopt, and comply with, the more stringent 14 CFR part 135 regulations required by the FAA for 14 CFR part 135 air carriers without having such a certificate. The NTSB is reassured by the position the FAA has taken in this manner, which supports a voluntary request from a public operator for a higher level of oversight.

At the time of the accident, MSP considered its medevac flights —civil aircraft operations operating under Part 91. A March 2008 memorandum from the commander to all personnel on the subject —Public Aircraft (Use) vs. Civil Aircraft (Part 91) Operations explained MSP's determination of which operations were —civil and which were —public. Review of the memorandum indicated that MSP made its determination by following the guidance provided in FAA AC 00-1.1, —Government Aircraft Operations. Per the guidance in the AC, the memorandum identified —medevac operations, VIP transports, training flights, mechanic transports, photo flights, etc. as —civil operations to be conducted in accordance with Part 91 and MSP policies and procedures. It identified —search and rescue missions and law enforcement support/homeland security operations, etc. as —public operations to be conducted in accordance with MSP policies and procedures. Further, the memorandum also followed the AC's guidance in stating that since MSP conducted both —civil and —public operations with the same aircraft, it was required to maintain its aircraft in accordance with the regulations applicable to civil aircraft in Parts 43 and 91.

---

[78] The legislature did conduct an audit of certain aspects of MSP's helicopter program in 2008; however, the scope of this audit did not include a review of aviation operational practices.

Prior to this accident, it appeared that the FAA also considered MSP's medevac flights to be civil, based on the FAA's published positions in AC 00-1.1 and Order 8900.1 and on a letter sent in 2000 from the FAA to a Part 135 HEMS operator, who requested an operational classification of MSP's interhospital patient transfers. In this letter, the FAA stated that assuming MSP's aircraft and pilots meet the requirements for civil aircraft operations, —so long as the MSP does not receive compensation from the hospital or patients for the air transportation portion of the interhospital transfers, these flights may be conducted as civil aircraft operations under Part 91. This statement is consistent with the guidance in Order 8900.1 regarding medevac flights that excludes the —routine medical evacuation of persons due to traffic accidents and other similar incidents or hospital-to-hospital transfers from the government function of search and rescue.

Despite the FAA's earlier opinion, during this accident investigation, the FAA provided to the NTSB a memorandum with a conflicting opinion on the operating status of MSP medevac flights. In this memorandum, dated March 13, 2009, the FAA stated that it believed the accident flight was a —public aircraft operation. The FAA supported its determination by referring to the definition of public aircraft in 49 U.S.C. section 40102(a)(41)(C) and the exception provided in 49 U.S.C. section 40125(b), which states that a government-owned aircraft does not qualify as a public aircraft —when it is used for commercial purposes or to carry an individual other than a crewmember or a qualified non-crewmember. The FAA indicated that since MSP does not operate its helicopters —for compensation or hire, Trooper 2 was not being used for commercial purposes. Further, the FAA indicated that the accident victims are considered to be —qualified non-crewmembers as they are individuals who are —associated with the performance of a governmental function.

The FAA did acknowledge in its memorandum that medevac flights are not specifically called out as an example of a governmental function in the statute. However, the FAA stated that it considered —helicopter emergency medical services as akin to the search and rescue' function used as an example in the statute and as falling within the statutory intent of governmental function. This new opinion is in direct contradiction with the guidance provided in FAA Order 8900.1 regarding medevac flights, which states that, —the term =search and rescue' does not include routine medical evacuation of persons due to traffic accidents and other similar incidents or hospital-to-hospital patient transfers. It is also in conflict with the guidance provided in AC 00-1.1, which states that the term —medical evacuation is not considered synonymous with —search and rescue. The FAA noted that it was aware of these contradictions and that —internal agency materials were being updated. As of the date of this writing, the guidance in FAA Order 8900.1 and AC 00-1.1 regarding medevac flights has not been revised.

The NTSB sees no basis for the FAA's determination that all medevac flights fall within the statutory intent of governmental function. Given that medevac flights are routinely conducted each day by numerous civilian operators, medevac cannot, as a general matter, be considered a governmental function. The NTSB finds persuasive the FAA's earlier guidance that routine medevac of persons due to traffic accidents or other similar incidents and hospital-to-hospital patient transfers are not governmental functions but that specific non-routine medevacs could be considered a governmental function if they meet specific criteria. Further, the NTSB notes that the earlier guidance provided in AC 00-1.1 and Order 8900.1 was comprehensive and consistent, whereas, to date, the FAA has provided no guidance beyond the March 13, 2009, memorandum regarding its new position.

The NTSB is especially concerned that the FAA's current position means that it does not consider patients carried by a public operator, such as MSP, to be passengers, but rather—qualified non-crewmembers. Many of the patients carried by EMS aircraft have sustained life-threatening traumatic injuries and are in no condition to make a decision about whether or not to be transported by air. If these patients are transported on a public aircraft, the FAA medical rules, aircraft certification requirements, pilot certifications, aircraft maintenance requirements and aircraft operator requirements do not apply, and the FAA provides no oversight and minimal surveillance of the operator. If the same patients are carried by a civilian aircraft, they would be considered passengers, the operator would be required to comply with the rules and requirements noted above, including the standards of 14 CFR Part 135, and the FAA would provide extensive oversight and surveillance of the operator. The patients carried by public EMS aircraft deserve the same level of safety as those carried on civil EMS aircraft.

Public Law 103-411 was enacted, in part, because Congress determined that government-owned aircraft that engage in transport of passengers should be subject to the regulations applicable to civil aircraft. Since the FAA has the statutory authority to regulate the operation and maintenance of civil aircraft but not public aircraft, the law redefined —public aircraft to exclude government-owned aircraft used for commercial purposes or engaged in the transport of passengers from operating as public aircraft. The purpose of this redefinition, as reflected in legislative history, was to mandate that FAA safety regulations, directives, and orders issued for civil aircraft be made applicable to all government-owned, nonmilitary aircraft engaged in passenger transport. The FAA's blanket classification of all medevac flights by government-owned aircraft operators as public operations does not appear to accord with the intent of Congress.

The NTSB concludes that the FAA's classification of all medevac flights by government-owned aircraft as public operations conflicts with its own earlier guidance, creates a discrepancy in the level of FAA safety oversight of HEMS aircraft operations carrying passengers, and is contrary to the intent of Public Law 103-411, which states that aircraft carrying passengers are excluded from operating as public aircraft. The NTSB recommends that the FAA seek specific legislative authority to regulate HEMS operations conducted using government-owned aircraft to achieve safety oversight commensurate with that provided to civil HEMS operations.

CHAPTER 4

CONCLUSIONS

Findings

1. The pilot was properly certificated and qualified in accordance with Maryland State Police standards. Additionally, although the Federal Aviation Administration classified the flight as a public operation, the pilot was qualified under 14 Code of Federal Regulations Part 91 to conduct the flight under visual flight rules or instrument flight rules as a civil operation.

2. The helicopter was properly certificated, equipped, and maintained in accordance with the requirements in 14 Code of Federal Regulations Parts 43 and 91 applicable to civil aircraft operating under visual flight rules or instrument flight rules. The recovered components showed no evidence of any preimpact structural, engine, or system failures.

3. Instrument meteorological conditions prevailed in the accident area with scattered clouds near 200 feet above ground level (agl) and cloud ceilings near 500 feet agl. Although Andrews Air Force Base was reporting visibility of 4 miles in mist, lower visibilities in fog occurred locally in the accident area.

4. The pilot's decision to accept the flight, after his inadequate assessment of the weather, contributed to the accident.

5. Had a formal flight risk evaluation program been in place at Maryland State Police before the accident, it may have resulted in the cancellation of the flight.

6. When the pilot was unable to reach Prince George's Hospital Center due to deteriorating weather conditions, he appropriately made the decision to divert to Andrews Air Force Base and request ground transport for the patients.

7. No evidence was found that suggests that the glideslope was not functioning properly. The lack of information regarding the accident airplane's navigation frequency settings and flight instrument indications precluded National Transportation Safety Board investigators from determining why the pilot believed he was not receiving a valid glideslope signal.

8. The pilot's workload increased substantially and unexpectedly as a result of encountering instrument weather conditions.

9. The pilot's expectation that he could descend below the cloud ceiling at an altitude above the minimum descent altitude for the approach, his familiarity with Andrews Air Force Base, and the reduction in workload a return to visual conditions would have provided are all factors that may have encouraged the pilot to deviate below the glideslope and attempt to —duck under the cloud ceiling.

10. The pilot failed to adhere to instrument approach procedures when he did not arrest the helicopter's descent at the minimum descent altitude.

11. Although descent rate and altitude information were readily

available through cockpit instruments, the pilot failed to monitor the instruments likely because he was preoccupied with looking for the ground, which he could not identify before impact due to the lack of external visual cues.

12. If the helicopter had been equipped with a terrain awareness and warning system, aural terrain alerts of —Caution Terrain,—Warning Terrain, and —Pull-up, would have been provided. These would have been more salient than the alert provided by the radar altimeter and likely would have caused the pilot to attempt to arrest his descent.

13. The failure of the Potomac Consolidated Terminal Radar Approach Control controller to provide the current Andrews Air Force Base weather information likely led the pilot to expect that he could descend below the cloud ceiling and establish visual contact with the ground at an altitude well above the minimum descent altitude for the approach.

14. Air traffic services provided by the Ronald Reagan Washington Airport Tower and Potomac Consolidated Terminal Radar Approach Control controllers to the accident flight exhibited numerous procedural deficiencies, including unresponsiveness, inattention, and poor radar vectoring. These deficiencies were a distraction to the pilot and increased his workload by requiring him to compensate for the poor services provided.

15. Although the pilot met the recent-experience requirements to act as pilot-in-command under instrument flight rules, he was not proficient in instrument flight. This lack of proficiency likely contributed to the pilot's failure to properly conduct what effectively became a non-precision approach at night in instrument conditions.

16. Changes made by the Maryland State Police Aviation Command to its instrument training program about 10 months before the accident did not promote instrument proficiency.

17. Based on the late hour, the length of time awake, the risk factors for sleep apnea exhibited by the pilot, and the decision to deviate from the published procedures, the pilot was likely less than fully alert, and fatigue may have contributed to his deficient decision-making.

18. The Maryland State Police System Communications Center duty officer lost situational awareness of the helicopter while it was in flight.

19. The lack of adherence to effective flight-tracking policies by Maryland State Police System Communications Center personnel created an institutional mindset that allowed duty officers to assume that aircraft had landed safely when the Automatic Dependent Surveillance- Broadcast signal was lost; over time, safe landings were taken for granted.

20. Had two Maryland State Police aviation employees not pursued their own search effort, locating the accident site would likely have taken several more hours than it did.

21. The incident commander's lack of aviation knowledge diminished the effectiveness of search and rescue activities.

22. Maryland State Police troopers and System Communications Center personnel were insufficiently equipped and trained to conduct a search involving global positioning system coordinates, and this hindered their ability to locate the site of the wreckage.

23. Neither Prince George's County nor Maryland State Police dispatchers fully understood the importance of obtaining distance and bearing information, as well as the cell tower location, before releasing a location obtained from cell phone pinging; this lack of understanding led dispatchers to provide the cell phone tower's simple street address without context to all units involved in the search. This distracted and confused units already searching a more likely location.

24. The Federal Aviation Administration air traffic control's inability to produce timely location data also hampered search and rescue efforts.

25. Knowledge of the disjointed search and rescue efforts and the techniques eventually employed to locate the accident site could provide valuable lessons to agencies, such as helicopter emergency medical services dispatch centers, 911 dispatch centers, and fire, police, and sheriff's departments, involved in search and rescue efforts.

26. Having aboard the aircraft a recorder system that captured cockpit audio, images, and parametric data would have aided the National Transportation Safety Board in determining the circumstances that led to this accident.

27. The Federal Aviation Administration's (FAA's) classification of all medical evacuation flights by government-owned aircraft as public operations conflicts with its own earlier guidance, creates a discrepancy in the level of FAA safety oversight of helicopter emergency medical services aircraft operations carrying passengers, and is contrary to the intent of Public Law 103-411, which states that aircraft carrying passengers are excluded from operating as public aircraft.

Probable Cause

The National Transportation Safety Board determines that

the probable cause of this accident was the pilot's attempt to regain visual conditions by performing a rapid descent and his failure to arrest the descent at the minimum descent altitude during a non-precision approach. Contributing to the accident were (1) the pilot's limited recent instrument flight experience, (2) the lack of adherence to effective risk management procedures by the Maryland State Police, (3) the pilot's inadequate assessment of the weather, which led to his decision to accept the flight, (4) the failure of the Potomac Consolidated Terminal Radar Approach Control (PCT) controller to provide the current Andrews Air Force Base weather observation to the pilot, and (5) the increased workload on the pilot due to inadequate Federal Aviation Administration air traffic control handling by the Ronald Reagan National Airport Tower and PCT controllers.

Key take aways:
- Proper weather Analysis
- Know and Follow procedures
- Currency and proficiency are two different things
- Dont be afraid to declare an emergency

CHAPTER 5

RECOMMENDATIONS

New Recommendations

As a result of this investigation, the National Transportation Safety Board makes the following safety recommendations:

To the Federal Aviation Administration:

Seek specific legislative authority to regulate helicopter emergency medical services (HEMS) operations conducted using government-owned aircraft to achieve safety oversight commensurate with that provided to civil HEMS operations. (A-09-130)

To All Public Helicopter Emergency Medical Services Operators:

Develop and implement flight risk evaluation programs that include training for all employees involved in the operation, procedures that support the systematic evaluation of flight risks, and consultation with others trained in helicopter emergency medical services flight operations if the risks reach a predefined level. (A-09-131)

Use formalized dispatch and flight-following procedures that include up-to-date weather information and assistance in flight risk assessment decisions. (A-09-132)

Install terrain awareness and warning systems on your aircraft and provide adequate training to ensure that flight crews are capable of using the systems to safely conduct helicopter emergency medical services operations. (A-09-133)

To the Maryland State Police:

Implement a program to screen and—if necessary—treat your pilots for obstructive sleep apnea. (A-09-134)

Revise your policy regarding incident commanders to specify that, in any event involving a missing or overdue aircraft, an Aviation Command trooper will serve as the incident commander. (A-09-135)

Provide additional training to your dispatchers on the use of cell phone —pinging and include instruction about how to integrate the data obtained from cell phone pinging into an overall search and rescue plan. (A-09-136)

To Prince George's County, Maryland:

Provide additional training to your dispatchers on the use of cell phone —pinging and include instruction about how to integrate the data obtained from cell phone—pinging into an overall search and rescue plan. (A-09-137)

To the National Association of Air Medical Communications Specialists, the Association of Public-Safety Communications Officials International, the National Emergency Number Association, the International Association of Police Chiefs, the National Sheriffs' Association, and the International Association of Fire Chiefs:

Inform your members through your websites, newsletters, and conferences of the lessons learned from the emergency response to this accident, particularly emphasizing that search and rescue personnel need to understand how to interpret and use both global positioning system coordinates and the results of cell phone—pinging. (A-09-138)

Previously Issued Recommendations Reiterated in this Report

The National Transportation Safety Board reiterates the following safety recommendations to the Federal Aviation Administration:

Require all emergency medical services (EMS) operators to develop and implement flight risk evaluation programs that include training all employees involved in the operation, procedures that support the systematic evaluation of flight risks, and consultation with others trained in EMS flight operations if the risks reach a predefined level. (A-06-13)

Require all rotorcraft operating under 14 Code of Federal Regulations Parts 91 and 135 with a transport-category certification to be equipped with a cockpit voice recorder (CVR) and a flight data recorder (FDR). For those transport category rotorcraft manufactured before October 11, 1991, require a CVR and an FDR or an onboard cockpit image recorder with the capability of recording cockpit audio, crew communications, and aircraft parametric data. (A-06-17)

Require all emergency medical services (EMS) operators to install terrain awareness and warning systems on their aircraft and to provide adequate training to ensure that flight crews are capable of using the systems to safety conduct EMS operations. (A-06-15)

APPENDIX

INVESTIGATION AND HEARING

Investigation

The National Transportation Safety Board (NTSB) was notified of the accident on the morning of September 28, 2008. NTSB investigators arrived on-scene later that day. Chairman Deborah A.P. Hersman was the Board member on-scene.

Parties to the investigation were the Federal Aviation Administration, Maryland State Police, American Eurocopter, and Turbomeca USA. In accordance with Annex 13 to the International Convention on Civil Aviation, an accredited representative from the Bureau d'Enquetes et d'Analyses was appointed to participate in this investigation.

Public Hearing

No public hearing was held for this accident.

Abbreviations and Acronyms

AC	advisory circular
ADS-B	automatic dependent surveillance-broadcast
ADW	Andrews Air Force Base
AFWA	Air Force Weather Agency
agl	above ground level
AIRMET	Airman's Meteorological Information
AOPA	Aircraft Owners and Pilots Association
ASOS	Automated Surface Observing System
ASR	airport surveillance radar
ATC	air traffic control
BMI	body mass index
CFR	*Code of Federal Regulations*
CVR	cockpit voice recorder
DCA	Ronald Reagan Washington National Airport
DME	distance measuring equipment
DO	duty officer
DoD	Department of Defense
DUAT	Direct User Access Terminal
EMS	emergency medical services
FAA	Federal Aviation Administration

FDR	flight data recorder
FICEMS	Federal Interagency Committee on Emergency Medical Servic
fpm	feet per minute
FSDO	flight standards district office
FY	fiscal year
GPS	global positioning system
HEMS	helicopter emergency medical services
Hg	Mercury
H-TAWS	helicopter terrain awareness and warning system
IFR	instrument flight rules
ILS	instrument landing system
IMC	instrument meteorological conditions
IPC	instrument proficiency check
LOC	localizer
MDA	minimum descent altitude
medevac	medical evacuation
MEL	minimum equipment list
METAR	meteorological aerodrome report
MIEMSS	Maryland Institute for Emergency Medical Services Systems
MSAW	minimum safe altitude warning
msl	mean sea level
MSP	Maryland State Police

NOTAM	notice to airmen
NTSB	National Transportation Safety Board
NWS	National Weather Service
PAR	power analyzer and recorder
PCT	Potomac Consolidated Terminal Radar Approach Control
PG	Prince George's
PGH	Prince George's Hospital Center
PIC	pilot-in-command
PIREPS	pilot weather reports
rpm	revolutions per minute
RVR	runway visual range
SYSCOM	System Communications Center
TAF	terminal aerodrome forecast
TAWS	terrain awareness and warning system
TIS-B	Traffic Information Service-Broadcast
U.S.C.	*United States Code*
VFR	visual flight rules
VMC	visual meteorological conditions

134

Other Air Crash Investigations:

On April 10, 2010 at 10:41 local time, approaching Runway 26 of Smolensk "Severny" airdrome, a Tupolev-154M aircraft of the State Aviation of the Republic of Poland crashed while conducting a non-regular international flight PLF 101 carrying passengers from Warsaw to Smolensk. The cause of the accident was the failure of the crew to take a timely decision to proceed to an alternate airdrome due to weather conditions at the airport of destination. All 96 persons on board, including Polish President Lech Kaczyński and his wife, died in the crash.

On 23 June 1985, Air India Flight 182, a Boeing 747-237B was on its way from Montreal, Canada, to London when it was blown up while in Irish airspace, and crashed into the Atlantic Ocean. 329 people perished. It was the largest mass murder in modern Canadian history. The explosion and downing of the carrier was related to the Narita Airport Bombing. Investigation and prosecution took 25 years. The suspects were members of the Sikh separatist Babbar Khalsa. Inderjit Singh Reyat, the only person convicted, was sentenced to 15 years in prison.

On Tuesday 25 July 2000 Air France Flight AFR 4590, a Concorde registered F-BTSC, took off from Paris Charles de Gaulle, to undertake a charter flight to New York with nine crew members and one hundred passengers on board. During takeoff from runway 26 right at Roissy Charles de Gaulle Airport, a tyre was damaged. A major fire broke out. The aircraft was unable to gain height or speed and crashed onto a hotel, killing all 109 people on board and 4 on the ground. The crash would become the end of the Concorde era.

On the 21st of December 1988, PANAM Flight 103, a Boeing 747-121, on its way from London Heathrow to New York, was blown up over the town of Lockerbie, Scotland. All 259 persons on board of the aircraft and 11 residents of the town of Lockerbie were killed. In 2001 the Libyan Megrahi was sentenced to life imprisonment in Scotland. In 2009 Megrahi applied to be released from jail on compassionate grounds. His appeal was granted and on the 20th of August 2009 he was released from prison. But was Megrahi really **guilty?**

On 31 May 2009, flight AF447, an Airbus A330-200, took off from Rio de Janeiro bound for Paris. At 2 h 10, a position message and some maintenance messages were transmitted by the ACARS automatic system. After this nothing was heard of from the aircraft. Six days later bodies and airplane parts were found by the French and Brazilian navies. All 228 passengers and crew members on board are presumed to have perished in the accident. A massive search by air and sea craft for the plane's black boxes failed so far.

On Sunday, March 27, 1977 KLM Flight 4805 and PANAM Flight 1736 both approached Las Palmas Airport in the Canary Islands, when a terrorist's bomb exploded on the airport. Both flights were diverted to the neighboring island of Tenerife. After Las Palmas Airport reopened first KLM Flight 4805 was cleared for takeoff, a few minutes later PANAM 1736 was cleared. Due to a number of misunderstandings both aircraft collided on the runway of Tenerife Airport during takeoff, killing 583 people.

AIR CRASH INVESTIGATIONS

THE PLANE THAT VANISHED
The Crash of Adam Air Flight 574

On 1 Januari 2007, a Boeing 737-4Q8, operated by Adam Air as flight DHI 574, was flying from Surabaya to Manado in Indonesia, when it suddenly vanished from radar. There were 102 people on board

George Cramoisi, Editor

On 1 January 2007, a Boeing 737-4Q8, operated by Adam Air as flight DHI 574, was on a flight from Surabaya, East Java to Manado, Sulawesi, at FL 350 (35,000 feet) when it suddenly disappeared from radar. There were 102 people on board.. Nine days later wreckage was found floating in the sea near the island of Sulawesi. The black boxes revealed that the pilots were so engrossed in trouble shooting the IRS that they forgot to fly the plane, resulting in the crash that cost the lives of all aboard.

AIR CRASH INVESTIGATIONS

PILOT ERROR KILLS 50 PEOPLE IN BUFFALO
The Crash of Colgan Air Flight 3407

Colgan Air Flight 3407, a Bombardier DHC-8-400, crashed 5 nautical miles before the international airport of Buffalo, New York, because of the captain's failure to manage the flight, killing all 49 people on board and one on the ground

Alistair Fitzgerald, editor

On February 12, 2009, about 2217 eastern standard time, Colgan Air, Flight 3407, a Bombardier DHC-8-400, on approach to Buffalo-Niagara International Airport, crashed into a residence in Clarence Center, New York, 5 nautical miles northeast of the airport. The 2 pilots, 2 flight attendants, and 45 passengers aboard the airplane were killed, one person on the ground was killed, and the airplane was destroyed. The National Transportation Safety Board determined that the probable cause of this accident was a pilot's error.

AIR CRASH INVESTIGATIONS

HARD LANDING KILLS 9
The Crash of Turkish Airlines Flight TK 1951 on Amsterdam Schiphol Airport

On 25 February 2009, Turkish Airlines flight 1951, a Boeing 737-800, with 135 people on board, was on its way from Istanbul in Turkey to Amsterdam Schiphol Airport in the Netherlands. Due to a malfunctioning radio altimeter and a failure to implement properly the stall recovery procedure the plane stalled and crashed just short of the runway of Schiphol Airport, killing 9 and injuring 120 people.

Igor Korsakov, editor

On 25 February 2009 a Boeing 737-800, flight TK1951, operated by Turkish Airlines was flying from Istanbul in Turkey to Amsterdam Schiphol Airport. There were 135 people on board. During the approach to the runway at Schiphol airport, the aircraft crashed about 1.5 kilometres from the threshold of the runway. This accident cost the lives of four crew members, and five passengers, 120 people sustained injuries. The crash was caused by a malfunctioning radio altimeter and a failure to implement the stall recovery procedure correctly.

On November 12, 2001, American Airlines flight 587, an Airbus A300-605R, took off from John F. Kennedy International Airport, New York. Flight 587 was a scheduled passenger flight to Santo Domingo, Dominican Republic, with a crew of 9 and 251 passengers aboard the airplane. Shortly after take-off the airplane lost its tail, the engines subsequently separated in flight and the airplane crashed into a residential area of Belle Harbor, New York. All 260 people aboard the airplane and 5 people on the ground were killed, and the airplane was destroyed by impact forces and a post crash fire.

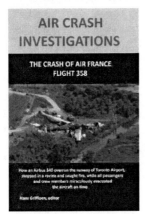

On August 2, 2005 Air France Flight 358, an Airbus A340, departed Paris, on a flight to Toronto, Canada, with 297 passengers and 12 crew members on board. On final approach, the aircraft's weather radar was displaying heavy precipitation. The aircraft touched down 3800 feet down the runway, and was not able to stop before the end of it. The aircraft stopped in a ravine and caught fire. All passengers and crew members were able to evacuate the aircraft on time. Only 2 crew members and 10 passengers were seriously injured during the crash and the evacuation.

On 2 September 1998, Swissair Flight SR 111 departed New York, flight to Geneva, Switzerland, with 215 passengers and 14 crew members on board. About 53 minutes after departure, the flight crew smelled an abnormal odour in the cockpit. They decided to divert to the Halifax International Airport. They were unaware that a fire was spreading above the ceiling in the front area of the aircraft. They did not make it to Halifax, 20 minutes later the aircraft crashed in the North Atlantic near Peggy's Cove, Nova Scotia, Canada. There were no survivors, 229 people died in the incident.

AIR CRASH INVESTIGATIONS

The Crash of Comair Flight 5191

How Comair Flight 5191, a Bombardier CL-600-2B19, took off from the wrong runway of Blue Grass Airport, Lexington, Kentucky, and crashed, killing 49 passengers and crewmembers

On August 27, 2006, Comair Flight 5191, a Bombardier CL-600-2B19, crashed during takeoff from the wrong runway of Blue Grass Airport, Lexington, Kentucky, killing 49 of the 50 people aboard. From the beginning everything went wrong. First the captain and first officer boarded the wrong airplane, only after starting the auxiliary power unit they found out they were in the wrong aircraft. Taxiing to the takeoff position the captain and first officer were so engaged in a private conversation that they did not realize they took the wrong runway. The air traffic controller did not notice anything.

AIR CRASH INVESTIGATIONS

The Crash of Helios Airways Flight 522

How crew and passengers of a Boeing 737 lost consciousness and crashed, after a long ghost flight, in the mountains of Greece, killing all 121 people on board

Hans Griffioen, editor

On 14 August 2005, a Boeing 737-300 aircraft departed from Larnaca, Cyprus, for Prague. As the aircraft climbed through 16.000 ft, the Captain contacted the company Operations Centre and reported a problem. Thereafter, there was no response to radio calls to the aircraft. At 07:21 h, the aircraft was intercepted by two F-16 aircraft of the Hellenic Air Force. They observed the aircraft and reported no external damage. The aircraft crashed approximately 33 km northwest of the Athens International Airport. All 121 people on board were killed.

AIR CRASH INVESTIGATIONS

The Crash of Aeroflot Flight 821

Unfamiliar instruments, lack of proper training and experience, fatigue and alcohol, became deadly ingredients for the crash of Aeroflot Flight 821, killing all 88 people aboard

Igor Korovin, editor

On 14 September 2008 Aeroflot Flight 821, a Boeing 737-505, operated by Aeroflot-Nord, a subsidiary of the Russian airline Aeroflot, crashed on approach to Bolshoye Savino Airport, Perm, Russia. All 82 passengers and 6 crew members were killed. The aircraft was completely destroyed. According to the final investigation report, the main reason of the crash was pilot error. Both pilots had lost spatial orientation, lack of proper training, insufficient knowledge of English and fatigue from lack of adequate rest. Alcohol in the Captain's blood may also have contributed to the accident.

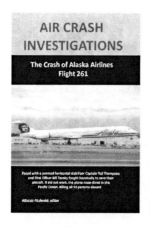

On January 31, 2000, Alaska Airlines, Flight 261, a McDonnell Douglas MD-83, was on its way from Puerto Vallarta, Mexico, to Seattle, Washington, when suddenly the horizontal stabilizer of the plane jammed. Captain Thompson and First officer Tansky tried to make an emergency landing in Los Angeles. The plane suddenly crashed into the Pacific Ocean, killing all 93 people aboard. The NTSB concluded that the crash was caused by insufficient maintenance. The crash of Alaska Airlines Flight 261 could have been avoided.

On May 11, 1996, at 1413:42 eastern daylight time, a Douglas DC-9-32 crashed into the Everglades 10 minutes after takeoff from Miami International Airport, Miami, Florida. The airplane was being operated by ValuJet Airlines, Inc., as flight 592 and was on its way to Atlanta, Georgia. Both pilots, the three flight attendants, and all 105 passengers were killed. The NTSB determined that the cause of the accident, was a fire in the airplane's cargo compartment, initiated by the actuation of an oxygen generator being improperly carried as cargo.

On August 24, 2001, Air Transat Flight 236, an Airbus 330, was on its way from Toronto, Canada to Lisbon, Portugal with 306 people on board. Above the Atlantic Ocean, the crew noticed a dangerous fuel imbalance. After flying 100 miles without fuel the crew managed to land the aircraft at the Lajes Airport at 06:45. Only 16 passengers and 2 cabin-crew members received injuries. The investigation uncovered a large crack in the fuel line of the right engine, caused by mistakes during an engine change just before the start of the flight.

On 19 December 1997 SilkAir Flight 185, a Boeing 737-300, operated by SilkAir, Singapore, on its way from Jakarta to Singapore, crashed at about 16:13 local time into the Musi river near Palembang, South Sumatra. All 97 passengers and seven crew members were killed. Prior to the sudden descent from 35,000 feet, the flight data recorders suddenly stopped recording at different times. There were no mayday calls transmitted from the airplane prior or during the rapid descent. The weather at the time of the crash was fine.

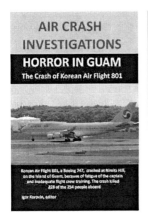

On August 6, 1997, about 0142:26 Guam local time, Korean Air flight 801, a Boeing 747-300, crashed at Nimitz Hill, Guam. The aircraft was on its way from Seoul, Korea to Guam with 237 passengers and a crew of 17 on board. Of the 254 persons on board, 228 were killed. The airplane was destroyed by impact forces and a post-crash fire. The National Transportation Safety Board determined that the probable cause of the accident was captain's fatigue and Korean Air's inadequate flight crew training.

This book explains the accident involving Atlantic Southeast Airlines flight 529, an EMB-120RT airplane, which lost a propeller blade and crashed near Carrollton, Georgia, on August 21, 1995. The accident killed 8 people on board. Safety issues in the report focused on manufacturer engineering practices, propeller blade maintenance repair, propeller testing and inspection procedures, the relaying of emergency information by air traffic controllers, crew resource management training, and the design of crash axes carried in aircraft.

142

Lauda Air Flight NG 104, a Boeing 767-300 ER of Austrian nationality was on a scheduled passenger flight Hong Kong-Bangkok-Vienna, Austria. NG 104 departed Hong Kong Airport on May 26, 1991, and made an intermediate landing at Bangkok Airport. The flight departed Bangkok Airport at 1602 hours. The airplane disappeared from air traffic radar at 1617 hours, about 94 nautical miles northwest of Bangkok. The probable cause of this accident is attributed to an uncommanded in-flight deployment of the left engine thrust reverser. All 223 people on board died in the accident.

On May 25, 1979, American Airlines Flight 191, a McDonnell-Douglas DC-10-10 aircraft, on its way from Chicago to Los Angeles, crashed just after take-off near Chicago-O'Hare International Airport, Illinois. During the take off the left engine and pylon assembly and about 3 ft of the leading edge of the left wing separated from the aircraft and fell to the runway. Flight 191 crashed killing two hundred and seventy one persons on board and two persons on the ground. The accident remains the deadliest airliner accident to occur on United States soil.

On August 12, 1985, a Japan Airlines B-747 aircraft lost, shortly after take-off, part of its tail and crashed in the mountains northwest of Tokyo. Of the 524 persons on board 520 were killed, 4 survived the accident. The accident was caused by a rupture of the aft pressure bulkhead of the aircraft, and the subsequent ruptures of a part of the fuselage tail, vertical fin and hydraulic flight control systems. The rupture happened as the result of an improper repair after an accident with the aircraft in Osaka, in June 1978.

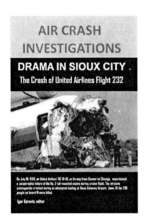

AIR CRASH INVESTIGATIONS

DRAMA IN SIOUX CITY

The Crash of United Airlines Flight 232

On July 19, 1989, an United Airlines' DC-10-10, on its way from Denver to Chicago, experienced a catastrophic failure of the No. 2 tail-mounted engine during cruise flight. The heroic pilots did all they could to bring the flight to a good end. But, notwithstanding all the attempts, the airplane subsequently crashed during an attempted landing at Sioux Gateway Airport, Iowa. Of the 296 people on board 111 were killed.

AIR CRASH INVESTIGATIONS

JAMMED RUDDER KILLS 132

The Crash of USAir Flight 427

The Boeing 737 has a history of rudder system-related anomalies, including numerous instances of jamming. During the course of the four and a half year investigation of the crash of USAir Flight 427 near Aliquippa, Pennsylvania, killing 132 people, the NTSB discovered that the PCU's dual servo valve could jam as well as deflect the rudder in the opposite direction of the pilots' input, due to thermal shock, caused when cold PCUs are injected with hot hydraulic fluid. This finally solved the mystery of sudden jamming of the rudders of this aircraft.

AIR CRASH INVESTIGATIONS

MYSTERIOUS CRASH KILLS 25

The Crash of United Airlines Flight 585

This amended report explains the accident involving United Airlines flight 585, a Boeing 737-200, on its way from Denver to Colorado Springs, which crashed on March 3, 1991 near Colorado Springs Municipal Airport. Only after the crash of USAir 427 in 1994 and a similar incident with Eastwind 517 in 1996 the NTSB was able to pinpoint the cause of this crash: jammed rudder. The Boeing 737 has a history of rudder system-related anomalies, this finally solved the mystery of sudden jamming of the rudders of this aircraft.

On October 31, 1999, EgyptAir flight 990, a Boeing 767-366ER crashed into the Atlantic Ocean 60 miles south of Nantucket, Massachusetts. All 217 people on board were killed, and the airplane was destroyed. The US National Transportation Safety Board determines that the probable cause of the accident is the airplane's departure from normal cruise flight and subsequent impact with the Atlantic Ocean as a result of the relief first officer's flight control inputs. The reason for the relief first officer's actions was not determined.

On October 31, 1999, EgyptAir flight 990, a Boeing 767-366ER crashed into the Atlantic Ocean 60 miles south of Nantucket, Massachusetts. All 217 people on board were killed, and the airplane was destroyed. Contrary to the conclusions of the American NTSB the Egyptian Investigation Team concludes that a mechanical defect is the most likely cause of the accident. According to the Egyptians there is no evidence to support a conclusion that the First Officer intentionally dove the airplane into the ocean in fact.

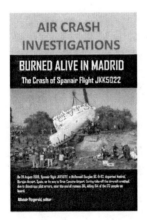

On 20 August 2008, Spanair flight JKK5022, a McDonnell Douglas DC-9-82 (MD-82), crashed during take-off from Barajas Airport in Madrid, The investigation revealed that the accident occurred as the aircraft attempted to take off, because the pilots had omitted to deploy the flaps and slats ready for take-off. The MD-82 warning system, that should have alerted the pilots that the plane was incorrectly configured for take-off, did not sound a warning. Of the 172 people on board 154 perished in the accident. Most burned alive.

On 25 January 2010, at 00:41:30 UTC, Ethiopian Airlines flight ET 409, a Boeing 737-800, on its way from Beirut to Addis Abeba, crashed just after take-off from Rafic Hariri International Airport in Beirut, Lebanon, into the Mediterranean Sea about 5 NM South West of Beirut International Airport. All 90 persons onboard were killed in the accident. The investigation concluded that the probable causes of the accident were pilot errors due to loss of situational awareness. Ethiopian Airlines refutes this conclusion.

On 4 October 1992, El Al Israel Airlines Flight 1862, a Boeing 747-200 Freighter, departed from Schiphol Airport, Amsterdam, on its way to Tel Aviv, Israel. Seven minutes after take-off the plane lost engine no. 3 and 4 and crashed in an apartment block just outside Amsterdam, killing 43 people (4 crewmembers and 39 on the ground). The investigation concluded that the design and certification of the B 747 pylon was inadequate to provide the required level of safety. Furthermore the system to ensure structural integrity by inspection failed.

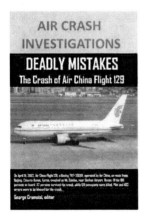

On April 15, 2002, about 11:21:17, Air China flight 129, a Boeing 767-200ER, operated by Air China, en route from Beijing, China to Busan, Korea, crashed on Mt. Dotdae, near Gimhae Airport, Busan. Of the 166 persons on board, 37 persons survived the crash, while 129 occupants were killed. The probable cause of the crash was pilot and ATC errors, while the airport did not inform the captain of the bad weather conditions at the time of landing in Busan. Because of these conditions eight previous flights were diverted to other airports.

On December 20, 1995, American Airlines Flight 965, a Boeing 757-223, was on a scheduled passenger flight from Miami, Florida, U.S.A., to Cali, Colombia. Close to its final destination the pilots erroneously cleared the approach waypoints from their navigation computer. When the controller asked the pilots to check back in over Tuluá, north of Cali, it was no longer programmed into the computer. They were lost and the aircraft crashed into a mountain. Of the 163 people on board, 4 passengers survived the accident.

On 25 December 2003, Union des Transport Aériens de Guinée Flight GIH 141, a Boeing 727-223, on a flight from Conakry (Guinea) to Kufra (Libya), Beirut (Lebanon) and Dubai (United Arab Emirates) stopped over at Cotonou, Republic of Benin. During takeoff the airplane, overloaded in an anarchic manner, was not able to climb properly and struck an airport building on the extended runway centerline, and crashed onto the beach, killing 151 of the 163 people on board. The crew was unknown with the forward center of gravity of the aircraft.

The Lockheed 1011 registered A6-BSM, chartered by Olympic Airlines, left as flight OA202 Charles de Gaulle International Airport, Paris, on 4 July 2005 at 16h18. Shortly after departure there were engine problems. The captain returned immediately. An investigation by the French BEA showed numerous technical problems with the aircraft, such as fuel and hydraulic leakages, non-working fire alarms and lack of maintenance. The flight crew was not properly licensed and the insurance was insufficient. In fact A6-BSM was a flying coffin.

On March 23, 2004, about 1918:34 central standard time, an Era Aviation Sikorsky S-76 helicopter, crashed into the Gulf of Mexico about 70 nautical miles south-southeast of Scholes International Airport (GLS), Galveston, Texas. The helicopter was en route to the drilling ship Discoverer Spirit. All 10 people aboard the helicopter were killed. The helicopter was destroyed. The probable cause of this accident was the flight crew's failure to identify and arrest the helicopter's descent which resulted in controlled flight into terrain.

During the night of 04th May 2007, the B737-800, registration 5Y-KYA, operated by Kenya Airways as flight KQA 507 from Abidjan international airport (Ivory Coast), to the Jomo Kenyatta airport Nairobi (Kenya), made a scheduled stop-over at the Douala international airport (Cameroon). Shortly after take-off at about 1000 ft, the aircraft entered into a slow right roll that increased continuously and eventually ended up in a spiral dive, the airplane crashed in a mangrove swamp, killing all 114 people aboard. The captain, as pilot flying, lost complete control.

On April 27, 1976, American Airlines Flight 625, a Boeing 727, during landing at the Harry S Truman Airport, Charlotte Amalie, St. Thomas, Virgin Islands, overran the end of runway 9, struck the ILS antenna, crashed through a fence, and hit a building located about 1,040 feet beyond the departure end of the runway. The aircraft was destroyed, 35 passengers and 2 flight attendants were killed. The National Transportation Safety Board determined that the probable cause of the accident was the captain's actions and his misjudgment during landing.

148

On 31 May 2009, the Airbus A330 flight AF 447 took off from Rio de Janeiro Galeào airport bound for Paris Charles de Gaulle. At 2h 10min 05, likely following the obstruction of the Pitot probes by ice crystals, the speed indications became incorrect and some automatic systems disconnected, the aeroplane came in a stall situation and crashed in the sea at 2 h 14 min 28s, killing all 228 persons on board. It took two years to recover the wreck of the aircraft from a depth of 4.000 metres. After two intermediate reports this is the final report of the crash.

On 2 May 2006 Armavia Flight RNV 967, an Airbus A320, was as a passenger flight on its way from Yerevan, Armenia to Sochi, Russia. Upon approaching Sochi there was confusion in regard to the cloud level and visibility for the scheduled landing. While trying to land the air traffic control ordered the captain to abort the landing. In the attempt to abort the captain lost control and the aircraft crashed in the sea, killing all 113 people on board. Contributing factors were not maintaining strict cockpit rules and deficiencies by air traffic control.

On September 27, 2008, an Aerospatiale (Eurocopter) SA365N1, call sign Trooper 2, operated by the Maryland State Police (MSP) as a public medical evacuation flight, encountered b ad weather en route to the hospital and was diverted to Andrews Air Force Base (ADW), Camp Springs, Maryland, 3.2 miles north of the runway 19R threshold at ADW, the helicopter impacted terrain and crashed. The commercial pilot, one flight paramedic, one field provider, and one automobile accident patients being transported were killed. The NTSB blamed the pilot's inexperience for the crash.

AIR CRASH
INVESTIGATIONS
FATIGUE?
The Crash of Federal Express Flight 1478

On July 26, 2002, about 0537 eastern daylight time, Federal Express flight 1478, a Boeing 727-232F, on its way from Memphis International Airport to Tallahassee Regional airport, struck trees on short final approach and crashed short of runway 9 at the Tallahassee Regional Airport, Florida. The captain, first officer, and flight engineer were seriously injured, and the airplane was destroyed. The National Transportation Safety Board determines that the probable cause of the accident was the crew's failure to establish and maintain a proper glidepath during the approach to landing.

AIR CRASH
INVESTIGATIONS
FAILING BRAKES
The Crash of TAM Linhas Aereas Flight 3054

On 17 July 2007 an Airbus A-320, operated as flight JJ3054 by the Brazilian company TAM Linhas Aéreas, was on its way from Porto Alegre, Brazil, for a domestic flight to Congonhas Airport in São Paulo city, Brazil. During the landing, the aircraft was not slowing down as expected, veered to the left, overran the left edge of the runway, crossed over the Washington Luís Avenue, and collided with a building, and with a fuel service station. All 187 persons on board and 12 people on the ground were killed in the accident.

AIR CRASH
INVESTIGATIONS
IN-FLIGHT ENGINE FAILURE
The Crash of Air Algerie Flight 6289

On Thursday 6 March 2003, Air Algérie Flight DAH 6289, a Boeing 737-200, suffered during take-off from Tamanrasset, in Southern Algeria, a contained burst in the left engine. The airplane swung to the left, lost speed progressively, stalled and crashed, with the landing gear still extended, about one thousand six hundred and forty-five meters from the takeoff point, to the left of the runway extended centerline. The crew and 96 passengers were killed in the accident, one passenger survived. The airplane was on a domestic flight from Tamanrasset to Ghardaïa and Algiers.

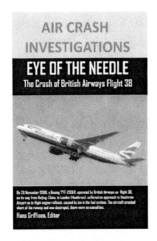

AIR CRASH INVESTIGATIONS

EYE OF THE NEEDLE
The Crash of British Airways Flight 38

On 28 November 2008, a Boeing 777-200ER, operated by British Airways as flight BA38, on its way from Beijing, China, to London (Heathrow), suffered on approach to Heathrow Airport an in-flight engine rollback. At 720 feet agl, both engines ceased responding to autothrottle commands. The result was that the aircraft touched down 330 m short of the paved surface of Runway 27L at London Heathrow. The reduction in thrust was due to restricted fuel flow to both engines, caused by the forming of ice in the fuel system. The aircraft was destroyed, but there were no casualties.

AIR CRASH INVESTIGATIONS

DEADLY MISTAKE
The Crash of Kish Airlines Flight IRK 7170

On February 10, 2004, Kish Airlines Flight IRK 7170, a Fokker F27, operated a scheduled passenger flight from Kish Island, Islamic Republic of Iran, to Sharjah, United Arab Emirates, a 35 minutes flight. During the approach of Sharjah International Airport, the aircraft was observed to pitch down and suddenly turn to the left. The aircraft continued to descend and turn at high pitch and roll angles and impacted a sandy area 2.6 nm from the runway threshold. A large explosion was seen. The aircraft was destroyed and there were 43 fatalities.

CPSIA information can be obtained
at www.ICGtesting.com
Printed in the USA
FFOW03n1303021017
40629FF